CW00520710

The Art of Poetry volume 8

Forward: *Poems of the Decade anthology*

Published by Peripeteia Press

First published Feb. 2017

ISBN: 97809954671-4-9

All rights reserved. No part of this publication may be reproduced, stored in a retrieval system or in any form or by any means, without the prior permission in writing of the publisher, nor otherwise circulated in any form or cover other than that which it is published and without a similar condition including this condition being imposed on the subsequent publisher.

Peripeteia.webs.com

Copyright Peripeteia Press

Contents

General Introduction to the The Art of Poetry series

The philosopher Nietzsche described his work as 'the greatest gift that (mankind) has ever been given'. The Elizabethan poet Edmund Spenser hoped his book *The Faerie Queene* would transform its readers into noblemen. In comparison, our aims for *The Art of Poetry* series of books are a little more modest. Fundamentally we aim to provide books that will be of maximum use to English students and their teachers. In our experience few students before A-level, and not all students at this level, read essays on poetry, yet, whatever specification they are studying, they have to write analytical essays on poetry. So, we've offering some models, written in a lively, challenging but accessible style.

This current book, volume 8, is dedicated to modern poetry and, in particular, to Edexcel's newly revised selection from the *Forward Poems of the Decade* anthology. Taken as a whole, we intend *The Art of Poetry* series to cover a rich and varied range of literature, from poems that have endured years of critical readings to ones on which very little has been written, until now that is.

Introduction to *volume 8: Poems of the Decade*

Squeezed into dingy corners of bookshops, squeezed almost entirely out of newspapers, squeezed thin to the point of invisibility in the media (with the honourable exception of radio 4) modern poets desperately need the oxygen of this rare exposure to a young, vibrant audience. Forward's *Poems of the Decade* anthology features a great, rich range of voices, styles, forms and views, and in its pages the reader discovers many of the most outstanding poetic voices of this generation, writing about the world around us now.

Edexcel examination board made a bold and commendable decision to make a modern poetry anthology a set text for both their new AS and A-level English Literature specifications. It's rare to see such an innovative text choice and we think there's something refreshing and invigorating about encountering literature that has not already been endlessly critiqued, discussed and argued over by academics and critics. These poems are not weighed down by critical baggage and neither therefore is the reader. Sometimes secondary sources can obscure our perceptions of the original texts. Reading a canonical poem students join the back of a very long queue of other readers. Reading and writing about Forward's anthology gives students and teachers the chance to stand right at the front and, with their own responses, to take part in shaping the emerging critical landscape around this anthology.

Being the first critics will be exciting, but it's also a challenging task. Performing the tight-rope walk of interpretation without the safety net of other readers can be daunting and make us feel exposed, uncertain of our bearings. In an examination situation, where the stakes are so high, the task might feel even more intimidating. We think some support might be welcome. The essays in this volume of *The Art of Poetry* are not intended to replace students' own reading of the poems; the fundamental job of an A-level English reader is to grapple with the set texts themselves and to construct their own readings from this direct interaction with the source material. Nor are these essays designed to provide model answers to be remembered and repeated in examination conditions. Rather they are meant as springboards; we hope they will stimulate discussion, that you will find things you agree with but also things with which you disagree. And, in both cases, interacting with our readings should help consolidate your own. So, these essays are sounding boards too against which you can test your own ideas. We'd like to say our essays are body boards too, because they're fun to ride/read and will carry you with their own momentum. But obviously that's an analogy that just takes things a bit too far. Overall, our hope is that reading these essays will lead you back into re-reading the poems themselves with greater avidity.

Our primary audience for this book is A-level students, but we've included teaching ideas that we hope might be of use to colleagues. (We've used the utterly unoriginal, but universally understood sign of the light bulb to signify a teaching idea. At the back of the book there's also a list of tried and tested revision activities which can be completed individually or with a class.) It's a brave step for English teachers to choose this anthology; there are no 'how to teach' guides or (currently) York Notes or such like, for this text; the onus is on the expertise and creativity of teachers to make this text work in a classroom. Fortunately, though I say it myself as a practising English teacher, English teachers enjoy this sort of creative challenge and are usually very good at them. A little support will, we hope, be useful.

Edexcel's exam questions require comparison of poems both at AS and A-level. At AS, students will have a choice of two questions, each of which will ask them to compare a poem of their choice with one chosen by the Edexcel examiners. Unsurprisingly, at A-level the task is a little stiffer. Here a poem from the Forward anthology will have to be compared with an 'unseen' poem. As teachers, we are well aware of the demands of writing about 'unseen' material, so in the next section of this introduction we offer some advice about how to tackle the unseen. We'll also say a few things about comparing texts.

Modern British poetry

To misquote Andrew Marvell just a little, had we but space enough and time we would, of course, provide a comprehensive overview of developments in British poetry from Thomas Hardy through to the most recently published work. Unfortunately, or perhaps, fortunately for you, we do not have the space or time to produce this here. And, to be honest, nor do A-level students or their teachers need a comprehensive literary context for *Poems of the Decade*. Marks in the Edexcel exam, will be rewarded for quality of reading and writing and for the strength of the comparison. There are no marks for context. Hence we have not written short potted biographies for each poet in the following essays. In any case, a little research on the internet will provide this information for the diligent student. If you are curious enough to want a comprehensive treatment, we strongly recommend *The Oxford English Literary History, volume 12, Part II*, by Randall Stevenson.

If there are no marks for context, why read this? Because context is always enriching. An understanding of the literary context deepens appreciation of any text. Context may not determine meanings, but it certainly has a significant effect. Consider, for instance, the following sentence, 'the duck is ready to eat'. How does the meaning of this sentence change if we change the context? If the context is a restaurant one meaning is clear. But a different meaning is evinced if the context is a pond. So, whether they are officially rewarded through assessment objectives or not, contexts (literary, socio-historical and of reception) are always significant.

Mainstream and the avant-garde

In all forms of art there is a mainstream and an avant-garde. After T. S. Eliot launched **The Waste Land** on an unsuspecting public in the 1920s and the Modernist Movement swept through the arts world a split opened up in English poetry that still, arguably, persists to this day. On one side were poets committed to the sort of radical thematic, stylistic and formal experimentalism that Modernism promoted. On the other were poets who wanted to ignore

Modernism and maintain the continuity with earlier, traditional English poetry.

Modernist texts are characterised by a bricolage, collage approach; structurally and linguistically they are fragmented. Generally interested in the mind and the workings of the subconscious such texts often explore topics traditionally seen as taboo. For example, in the novel, Modernists develop the 'stream of consciousness' to reveal the subconscious drives governing characters' behaviour. Often drawing on classical literature as a form of ironic intertextual contrast, Modernist works also tend to be self-reflexive - in dialogue with themselves and their own procedures. And, as anyone who has read *The Waste Land* or tried to read James Joyce's seminal Modernist novel, *Ulysses,* will know all too well, Modernist texts tend to be hard to understand and their subject matter challenging. Consider, for instance, Picasso's famous painting *Les Demoiselles d'Avignon*, first exhibited in 1907, and a prime example of early Modernism in the visual arts:

Not exactly a conventional depiction of the female nude, is it?

In contrast, traditionalist poets eschewed what they considered to be the self-

indulgent excesses, elitism and brain-bending difficulties of Modernism, valuing instead well-crafted, sonorous and coherent poems which aimed to communicate comprehensible meaning to a wider audience. Focusing on capturing 'the real', antipathetic to anything smacking of redundant Romanticism, illogical mysticism or foreign fancy avant-gardism, these poets championed traditional craft skills of writing, embodied for them in the work of the Victorian poet, Thomas Hardy, pictured here. In the 1950s and 60s a group of poets developed who gave the emphasis on well-made poems a contemporary, down-to-earth, restrained, peculiarly English spin. Known as **The Movement** poets, they developed a poetic aesthetic that dominated the mainstream of English poetry for many decades. Arguably, indeed, their ideas still have a powerful influence on contemporary poetry.

Movement poets often took an ironic observatory role to comment on the vagaries of modern culture. Often they combined traditional, regular poetic forms with modern, colloquial English and arch references to popular culture. Philip Larkin is the most famous poet associated with The Movement. Though other strains kicked against this mainstream, notably the work of Ted Hughes and Sylvia Plath and, in America, the rhapsodic style of the Beat poets, Movement aesthetic, as we have said, persisted into the late twentieth century as the dominant one in English poetry.

The approach of the other side of the divide was well articulated by Iain Sinclair in the provocative introduction to his radical anthology of English poetry, which, even in its title sticks a metaphorical two fingers up to The

Movement and its followers. Sinclair's anthology **Conductors of Chaos** was first published in 1996. Here's a taste of the introduction:

> The work I value is that which seems most remote, alienated, fractured. I don't claim to 'understand' it but I like having it around. The darker it grows outside the window, the worse the noises from the island, the more closely do I attend to the mass of instant-printed pamphlets that pile up around my desk. The very titles are pure adrenalin: *Satyrs and Mephitic Angels, Tense Fodder, Hellhound Memos, Civic Crime, Alien Skies, Harpmest Intermezzi, A Pocket History of the Soul.* You don't need to read them, just handle them: feel the sticky heat creep up through your fingers.... Why should they be easy? Why should they not reflect some measure of the complexity of the climate in which they exist? Why should we not be prepared to make an effort, to break sweat, in hope of high return?

Sinclair goes on to offer some interesting advice on how to read any poem, but especially a radical, avant-garde one:

> There's no key, no Masonic password: take the sequence gently, a line at a time. Treat the page as a block, sound it for submerged sonar effects. Suspend conditioned reflexes...if it comes too sweetly, somebody is trying to sell you something.

Try placing all the set poems in the Forward Anthology on a continuum from, at one end, avant-garde/ radical/ experimental and at the other end mainstream/ traditional/ well-made. Repeat the exercise, only this time arrange the poems by their various constituent elements, form, language, themes. Some poems, might, for instance, be radical in terms of content, but more conventional in form, or vice versa. At the end of this process you should develop a sense of which poem is the most radical and which the most traditional in approach. Which is better, or, indeed, whether one style is better than another, is for you to judge.

Tackling the unseen

If Literature is a jungle, of all the beasts that roam or lurk among its foliage, from the enormous, lumbering Victorian state-of-the-nation novel to the carnivorous revenge tragedy, the most dangerous by far is a small, fast-moving beast, a beast un-tethered by place or time, a beast that is, in fact invisible. This infamous critter is called, simply, 'the unseen'.

Well, that's sounds all rather alarming. Let's bring the rhetoric down a notch or ten. How should you go about analysing an unseen poem and how can you prepare for this demanding task?

To start with, we don't believe that there's one universally right method for reading poems. If there were, all the varied types of literary theorists - Feminist, Marxist, poststructuralist, postcolonial and so on - would have to adopt the same working methods. And, like the children depicted below, critics and theorists do not all read in the same way. So, it's vital to appreciate that there's no single master key that will unlock all poems.

A uniformly applicable method of reading a poem, or of writing about it in an examination, or for coursework, is like the philosopher's stone; it just does not exist. Or as Iain Sinclair puts it, there's no 'Masonic password' that will give you instant access to the inner chamber of a poem's secret meanings.

Having a singular method also makes the foolish assumption that all poems can be analysed in exactly the same way. A mathematician who thinks all maths problems can be solved with one method probably won't get very far, we expect. Instead you need to be flexible and trust your own trained reading skills. Respond to the key features of the text that is in front of you as you see them. It's no good thinking you will always write your second paragraph on figurative imagery, for instance, because what are you going to do when confronted with a poem entirely devoid of this feature? Although all the essays in this book explore key aspects of poetry, such as language, form, themes, effects and so forth, we haven't approached these aspects in a rigid, uniform or mechanical way. Rather our essays are shaped by what we found most engaging about each poem. For some poems this may be the use the poet has made of form; for others it might be imagery; for others still it might be the way the poet orchestrates language to bring out its musical properties. In terms of critical approach, we'd champion well-informed freedom above over-regulated and imposed conformity. Hence, we hope our essays will be varied and interesting and a little bit unpredictable, a bit like the poems themselves. We trust that if you write about how a poet's techniques contribute to the exploration of themes and generation of effect you won't be going far wrong.
(If you're interested in trying different methods of analysing poems, there is a concise guide in our A-level companion book, *The Art of Writing English Literature essays, for A-level and Beyond*).

So, to reiterate: Always keep to the fore of your essay the significance and impact of the material you're analysing. Very sophisticated analysis involves exploring how different aspects of the poem work in consort to generate effects. As a painter uses shapes, brush strokes, colours and so forth, or a composer uses chords, notes and time signatures, so a poet has a range of poetic devices at his or her disposal.

Think of a poem as a machine built to remember itself. Your task is to take apart the poem's precision engineering - the various cogs, gears and wheels that make the poem go - and to examine carefully how they work. If you can also explain how they combine to generate the poem's ideas and feelings you will, without a shadow of a doubt, achieve top marks.

We believe your essays must express your own thoughts and feelings, informed by the discipline of literary study and by discussion with your teachers and peers. And, that your essays should be expressed in your own emerging critical voice. Finding, refining and then trusting your critical voice is part of the self-discovery that contributes to making English Literature such a rewarding subject to study at A-level.

Offering quality support material, a safety net, if you like, for your walk on the tightrope of interpretation, we hope to give you confidence to make it across to the other side. And in achieving this, to also achieve great grades in your exams.

Writing comparative essays

The following is adapted from our discussion of this topic in *The Art of Writing English Literature Essays* course companion book, and is a briefer, nuts and bolts version, tailored to the Edexcel exam task. Fundamentally comparative essays want you to display not only your ability to intelligently talk about literary texts, but also your ability to make meaningful connections between them. The first starting point is your topic. This must be broad enough to allow substantial thematic overlapping of the texts. However, too little overlap and it will be difficult to connect the texts; too much overlap and your discussion will be lopsided and one-dimensional. In the case of the Edexcel exam, the board will determine the topic they want you to discuss. The exam question will ask you to focus on the methods used by the poets to explore a particular theme. You will also be directed to write specifically on themes, language and imagery as well as other poetic techniques.

One poem from the set text will be specified. You will then have to choose a companion poem. Selecting the right poem for interesting comparison is obviously very important. To think about this visually, you don't want Option A, below, [not enough overlap] or Option B [two much overlap]. You want Option C. This option allows substantial common links to be built between your chosen texts where discussion arises from both fundamental similarities AND differences.

Option A: too many differences

Option B: too many similarities

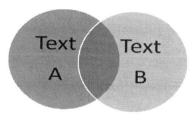

Option C: suitable number of similarities and differences

The final option will generate the most interesting discussion as it will allow substantial similarities to emerge as well as differences. The best comparative essays actually find that what seemed like clear similarities become subtle differences and vice versa while still managing to find rock solid similarities to build their foundations on.

How should you structure your comparative essay? Consider the following structures. Which one is best and why?

Essay Structure #1

1. Introduction
2. Main body paragraph #1 - Text A
3. Main body paragraph #2 - Text A
4. Main body paragraph #3 - Text B
5. Main body paragraph #4 - Text B
6. Conclusion

Essay Structure #2

1. Introduction
2. Main body paragraph #1 - Text A
3. Main body paragraph #2 - Text A
4. Main body paragraph #3 - Text B
5. Main body paragraph #4 - Text B
6. Comparison of main body paragraphs #1 & #3 - Text A + B
7. Comparison of main body paragraphs #2 & #4 - Text A + B
8. Conclusion

Essay Structure #3

1. Introduction
2. Main body paragraph #1 - Text A + B
3. Main body paragraph #2 - Text A + B
4. Main body paragraph #3 - Text A + B
5. Main body paragraph #4 - Text A+ B
6. Conclusion

We hope you will agree that 3 is the optimum option. Option 1 is the dreaded 'here is everything I know about text A, followed by everything I know by Text B' approach where the examiner has to work out what the connections are between the texts. This will score the lowest AO4 marks. Option 2 is better: There is some attempt to compare the two texts. However, it is a very inefficient way of comparing the two texts. For comparative essay writing the most important thing is to discuss both texts together. This is the most effective and efficient way of achieving your overall aim. Option 3 does this by comparing and contrasting the two texts under common umbrella headings. This naturally encourages comparison. Using comparative discourse markers, such as 'similarly', 'in contrast to', 'conversely' 'likewise' and 'however' also facilitates effective comparison.

When writing about each poem keep the bullet points in mind. Make sure you do not work chronologically through a poem, summarising the content of each stanza. Responses of this sort typically start with 'In the first stanza' and employ discourse markers of time rather than comparison, such as 'after', 'next', 'then' and so forth. Even if your reading is analytical rather than summative your essay should not work through the poem from the opening to the ending. Instead, make sure you write about the ideas explored in both texts (themes), the feelings and effects generated and the techniques the poet's employ to achieve these.

Writing about language

Poems are paintings as well as windows: We look at them as well as through them. As you know, we have to pay special attention to language in poetry because of all the literary art forms poetry, in particular, employs language in a self-conscious and distinctive way. We can break down the analysis of language into a number of different categories:

- By **diction** we mean the vocabulary used in a poem. A poem might be composed from the ordinary language of everyday speech or it might use elaborate, technical or elevated phrasing. Or both.
- **Grammatically** a poem may use complex sentences, or employ a lot of adjectives. Or it may rely extensively on nouns and verbs connected in simple sentences. Picking out and exploring words from specific grammatical classes has the merit of being incisive and usually illuminating.
- Poets might mix together different types, conventions and registers of language, moving, for example, between formal and informal, spoken and written, and so forth. Arranging the diction in the poem in terms of **lexico-semantic fields**, by register or by etymology, helps reveal these underlying patterns of meaning.
- For almost all poems **imagery** is a crucial aspect of language. Broadly imagery is a synonym for description and can be broken down into two types, **sensory and figurative**. Figurative imagery, in particular, is always significant. Not all poems rely on metaphors and similes; these devices are only part of a poet's repertoire, but figurative language is always important when it occurs because it compresses multiple meanings into itself. To use a technical term figurative images are polysemic, they contain many meanings. Try writing out the all the meanings contained in a metaphor in a more concise and economical way. Even simple, everyday metaphors compress meaning in this way. If we want to say our teacher is fierce and powerful and that we fear his or her wrath, we can more concisely say our teacher is a monster.

Writing about patterns of sound

What not to do: Tempting as it may be to spot sonic features of a poem and list these, don't do this. Avoid something along the lines of "The poet uses alliteration here and the rhyme scheme is ABABCDCDEFEFGG." Sometimes, indeed, it may be tempting to set out the poem's whole rhyme scheme like this. Resist the temptation: This sort of identification of features is worth zero marks. Marks in exams are reserved for attempts to link techniques to meanings and to effects.

Probably many of us have been sitting in English lessons listening somewhat sceptically as our English teacher explains the surprisingly specific significance of some seemingly random piece of alliteration in a poem. Something along the lines "The double d sounds here reinforce a sense of invincible strength" or "the harsh repetition of the 't' sounds suggests anger". Through all of our minds at some point may have passed the idea that, in these instances, English teachers appear to be using some sort of Enigma-style secret symbolic decoding machine that reveals how particular patterns of sounds have such particular coded meanings.

And this sort of thing is not all nonsense. Originally deriving from an oral tradition, poems are, of course, written for the ear as much as for the eye, to be heard as much as read. A poem is a soundscape as much as it is a set of meanings. Sounds are, however, difficult to tie to very definite meanings and effects. By way of example, the old BBC radiophonic workshop, which produced ambient sounds for radio and television programmes, used the same sounds in different contexts, knowing that the audience would perceive them in the appropriate way because of that context. Hence the sound of bacon sizzling, of an audience clapping and of feet walking over gravel were actually recordings of an identical sound. Listeners heard them differently because of the context. So, we may, indeed, be able to spot the repeated 's' sounds in a poem, but whether this creates a hissing sound like a snake or the susurration of the sea will depend on the context within the poem and the ears of the reader. Whether a sound is soft and soothing or harsh and grating is also open to interpretation.

The idea of connecting these sounds to meanings or significance is also a good one. Your analysis will be most convincing if you use a number of pieces of evidence together. In other words, rather than try to pick out individual examples of sonic effects we recommend you explore the weave or pattern of sounds, the effects these generate and their contribution to feelings and ideas. For example, this might mean examining how alliteration and assonance are used together to achieve a particular mimetic effect. An example will help demonstrate what we mean.

In John Burnside's poem, *History,* he describes bits and bobs of debris found on a beach in the following way:

Snail shells, shreds of razorfish;
Smudges of weed and flesh on tideworn stone

Sonically, fragile detritus is made to appear solid and significant. Sibilance connects many of the words together. The cohesive sonic effect this generates is re-enforced by the weave of other sounds:

- soft 'sh' sounds
- alliteration of 'w'
- assonance of 'a' s and of 'e's, the latter lengthen to 'ee' in 'weed'
- consonantal half rhyme of 'fish' and 'flesh'.
- a 'dge' rhyme sound carried from 'shreds' to 'smudge'

In concert, a rich, musical soundworld is constructed. The effect here is clear; to appreciate the full significance you'll need to read the essay on this poem.

Writing about form & structure

As you know by now, there are no marks for simply identifying textual features. This holds true for language, sounds and for form. Consider the relationship between a poem's form and its themes and effects. Broadly speaking the form can either work with or against a poem's content. Conventionally a sonnet, for instance, is about love, whereas a limerick is a comic form. A serious love poem in the form of a limerick would be unusual.

Start off taking a panoramic perspective: Think of the forest, not the trees. Don't even read the words, just look at the poem on the page, like a painting. Is the poem slight, thin, fat, long, short? What is the relation of whiteness to blackness? A poem about a long winding river will probably look rather different from one about a small pebble. Think, for instance, about how Eavan Boland uses form in *Inheritance* to convey a sense of contemplative thought. How does the visual layout of the poem relate to what it is about? Does this form enhance or create a tension against the content? Is the form one you can recognise, like a sonnet?

Zoom in: Explore the stanza form, lineation, enjambment and caesura. Focus in on specific examples and on points of transition. For instance, if a poem has four regular quatrains followed by a couplet examine the effect of this change. Consider regularity. Closed forms of poems, such as sonnets, are highly regular with set rhyme schemes, metre and number of lines. The opposite form is called 'open', the most extreme version of which is free verse. In free verse poems the poet dispenses with any set metre, rhyme scheme or recognisable traditional form. Try placing the poems from the Forward anthology on a continuum from regular to irregular, from closed to free verse.

Nice to metre...

A brief guide to metre and rhythm in poetry

Why express yourself in poetry? Why read words dressed up and expressed as a poem? What do can you get from poetry that can't from prose? There are many compelling answers to these questions. Here, though, we're going to concentrate on one aspect of the unique appeal of poetry – the structure of sound in poetry. Whatever our stage of education, we are all already sophisticated at detecting and using structured sound. Try reading the following sentences without any variation whatsoever in how each sound is  emphasised, and they will quickly lose what essential human characteristics they have. The sentences will sound robotic. So, in a sense, we won't be teaching anything new here. It's just that in poetry the structure of sound is carefully unusually crafted and created. It becomes a key part of what a poem is.

We will introduce a few new key technical terms along the way, but the ideas are straightforward. Individual sounds (syllables) are either stressed (emphasised, sounding louder and longer) or unstressed. As well as clustering into words and sentences for meaning, these sounds (syllables) cluster into rhythmic groups or feet, producing the poem's metre, which is the characteristic way its rhythm works.

In some poems the rhythm is very regular and may even have a name, such as iambic pentameter. At the other extreme a poem may have no discernible regularity at all. As we have said, this is called free verse. It is vital to remember that the sound in a good poem is structured so that it combines effectively with the meanings.

For example, take a look at these two lines from Marvell's *To his Coy Mistress*:

'But at my back I alwaies hear
Times winged Chariot hurrying near:'

Forgetting the rhythms for a moment, Marvell is basically saying at this point 'Life is short, Time flies, and it's after us'. Now concentrate on the rhythm of his words.

- In the first line every other syllable is stressed: 'at', 'back', 'al', 'hear'.
- Each syllable before these is unstressed 'But', 'my', 'I', 'aies'.
- This is a regular beat or rhythm which we could write ti TUM / ti TUM / ti TUM / ti TUM , with the / separating the feet. ('Feet' is the technical term for metrical units of sound)
- This type of two beat metrical pattern is called **iambic**, and because there are four feet in the line, it is **tetrameter**. So this line is in 'iambic tetrameter'. (Tetra is Greek for four)
- Notice that 'my' and 'I' being unstressed diminishes the speaker, and we are already prepared for what is at his 'back', what he can 'hear' to be bigger than him, since these sounds are stressed.
- On the next line, the iambic rhythm is immediately broken off, since the next line hits us with two consecutive stressed syllables straight off: 'Times' 'wing'. Because a pattern had been established, when it suddenly changes the reader feels it, the words feel crammed together more urgently, the beats of the rhythm are closer, some little parcels of time have gone missing.

A physical rhythmic sensation is created of time slipping away, running out. This subtle sensation is enhanced by the stress-unstress-unstress pattern of words that follow, 'chariot hurrying' (TUM-ti-ti, TUM-ti-ti). So the hurrying sounds underscore the meaning of the words.

13 ways of looking at a poem

1. Crunch it (1) – This means re-ordering all of the text in the poem under grammatical headings of nouns, verbs, prepositions and so forth. If this is done before reading the poem for the first time, the students' task is (a) to try to create a poem from this material and (b) to work out what they can about the style and themes of the original poem from these dislocated grammatical aspects. An alternative is to list the words alphabetically and do same exercise. You'll see we suggest something along these lines for Simon Armitage's poem. Re-arranging the poem in grammatical categories after reading can also be a useful analytical task.

2. Crunch it (2) – This is another exercise that can be used as an introductory activity before reading a poem for the first time or as a useful revision task. Rearrange the poem into groupings based on lexico-semantic fields. Show students one group of words at a time, asking them to write down what each group of words might tell us about the poem's themes & style. Alternatively, split the class into small groups and give each one group of words. Ask them to suggest possible titles for the poem.

3. Crunch it (3) – In this method students have to reduce each line of the poem to one key word. If they do this individually, then in pairs, then as a class, it can facilitate illuminating whole class discussion and bring out different readings. We've applied the cruncher at the end of each of the following essays.

4. Cloze it (aka blanket-blank) – A cloze exercise helps students to focus on specific choices of vocabulary. Blank out a few important words in the first couple of stanzas and as much as you dare of the rest of the

poem. Make this task harder as the course goes on. Or use it for revision to see how well the poem's been remembered.

5. Shuffle it – Give students all the lines in the poem but in the wrong order. Their task is to find the right order. Make this a physical exercise; even older pupils like sticking cut up pieces of paper together! Start off with reasonably easy activities. Then make them fiendishly hard.

6. Split it – Before a first reading, post a few key lines from the poem around the classroom, like clues for literary detectives. Arrange the class into small groups. Each group analyses only a few lines. Feedback to the class what they have found out, what they can determine about the poem. Ask them how the information from other groups confirms/ changes their thoughts. Finish by getting them to sequence the lines.

7. Transform it – Turn the poem into something else, a storyboard for a film version, a piece of music or drama, a still image, a collage of images, a piece of performance art. Engage your and their creativity.

8. Switch it – Swap any reference to gender in the poem and the gender of the poet. Change every verb or noun or metaphor or smile in the poem. Compare with the non-doctored version; what's revealed?

9. Pastiche or parody it – Ask students to write a poem in the style of one of the poems from the anthology. Take printed copies in. Add your own and one other poem. See if the students can recognise the published poem from the imitations. A points system can add to the fun.

10. Match it (1) – Ask students to find an analogue for the poem. Encourage them to think metaphorically. If they think Burnside's *History* is like a thrash metal song by the *The Frenzied Parsnips* they'll really need to explain how.

11. Match it (2) – Take some critical material on about 5 or 6 poets; there's good stuff on the **Poetry by Heart** and Poetry Archive websites. Take one poem by each of these poets and a photo. Mix this material up on one page of A3. The students' task is to match the poet to the critical material and to the image. To add to the creative fun you could make up a poem, poet and critical comments.

12. Complete it - Give the students the first few lines of the poem. Their task is to complete it. If they get stuck and plead profusely and if you're feeling especially generous, you can give them a few clues, such as the rhyme scheme or the stanza form.

13. Write back to - If the poem's a dramatic monologue, like Patience Agbabi's *Eat Me* change the point of view and write the man's version of events. What might be the silent hunter's thoughts in Vicki Feaver's *The Gun*?

14. Listen to it - Tell the class you're going to read the poem once. Their task is to listen carefully and then write down as much of it as they can remember, working first on their own and then in pairs. Read the poem a second time and repeat the exercise. Discuss what they did and didn't remember.

Yes, we know that's 14 things to do with a poem. Think of the last one as a bonus.

'Poetry's real work in human life and in culture is the magnification and clarification of being.'

JANE HIRSHFIELD

David Herd: *The Importance of the Title*

The shortest poem in the anthology is not on the Edexcel set list. But it makes for a good lesson starter activity on the significance of titles.

The poem is by academic & poet David Herd and is just two lines long:

Worked in the morning.
Watched TV.

What can we say about such a short, seemingly inconsequential poem? How could it possibly have been selected from all the other hundreds of poems for *Forward Poems of the Decade*? Is this, perhaps, another example of the sort of craziness that often gives modern art such a bad name? Is it, maybe, some sort of game about how we construct a poem by reading it as such? Could it just as easily have been:

Maybe some sort of game.
About how we construct
A poem by reading it as such.

Let's suppress our inner Daily Mail-appalled-common-sense reader for a moment and give the poet and the anthologisers the benefit of the doubt, for now, at least and treat the two lines of the poem to the same level of analysis as would to any literary masterwork. Clearly the poem is composed of very ordinary, everyday language and outlines a very ordinary, seemingly insignificant experience. Probably most of us do this or something like this each day and few of us would think of writing a poem about something so utterly mundane. And if we did, we'd probably be tempted to try and jazz it up a bit. But, there are none of the usual poetic techniques, such as imagery or sonic effects, here. Both of the two sentences are incomplete fragments, denuded of a subject, which we take to be 'I'. This helps create the impression of someone speaking, perhaps. They are blunt, truncated and seemingly plain statements of fact - technically both sentences are declaratives. Plainness of language matches the ordinary experience. But so what? We could say the same for the language on a bus ticket.

So, let's keep at it: Each of the two lines ends with an emphatic full stop, so that the two experiences of work and leisure seem disconnected. Maybe there's the suggestion that only these two things mattered for some reason. Why, for instance, aren't there further lines outlining other quotidian experiences, such as 'drank some tea', 'drove home', 'cooked the dinner'? So, something about watching the TV at this point must have been very important.

After spending as long as you or your class can stomach on analysing the poem's six words, the next task is to suggest possible titles for the poem. Here are a few my cynical year 11 class suggested: *Life, School, What I learnt today, The shortest poem with the longest possible title we could think of.* Once the class have tired of this you can reveal the poem's actual title: **September 11th, 2001**. Now discuss what difference the title makes.

Patience Agbabi: *Eat Me*

1.

In terms of form, Agbabi's poem is a dramatic monologue written in the voice of an obese woman kept in some sort of captivity by a perverse male lover. According to **The Oxford Companion of English Literature** a dramatic monologue is a poem 'delivered as though by a single imagined person, frequently but not always to an imagined auditor: the speaker is not to be identified with the poet, but is dramatised, usually ironically, through his or her own words'. The Companion goes on to note that the Victorian poet Robert Browning was especially adept at this form (Browning's **My Last Duchess** - which will feature in a forthcoming *The Art of Poetry* book - is one of his finest dramatic monologues). The key ideas here are that we have a character speaking, not the poet, and that irony is a key device in dramatic monologues. In particular, there is usually an ironic gap between what the central character says about themselves and what the writer implies. We'll keep this idea in mind when we explore character in more detail.

Still thinking in terms of classification, how else might we classify it? Thematically it's a sort of love poem, albeit a perverse one, and it also has a strong narrative element. It reminds me a little of a parable or a moral fable. Like the story of King Midas, it warns of the dangers of greed. There's something of Ovid's story of Erysichthon who desecrates a sacred grove and is cursed by the Goddess Ceres to suffer such insatiable hunger that he ends up eating himself. Agbabi's use of religious language of 'forbidden fruit', her monstrous characters and the comeuppance of the greedy man suggests to me that she wanted a sort of mythic dimension to her modern fable or urban myth.

2.

How does the protagonist present herself?

- 'When I hit thirty' suggests her age, especially in conjunction with the reference to 'cake'. However we soon realise that this refers to her morbid obesity. That rather indirect way of telling us her weight might imply some embarrassment or shame at her condition
- She's submissive to the man, at least at first: she 'did/ what' she 'was told' even when it brings her no pleasure; parading herself, she seems to do the man's bidding
- She's treated as an object and a possession, an assembly of parts - a 'belly', 'chins' & 'hips'
- A series of metaphors dehumanise her and express her identity in terms of the pleasure she provides for the male character: 'I was his Jacuzzi'; 'forbidden fruit" 'breadfruit'; 'a beached whale on a king-size bed'; 'a tidal wave of flesh'; 'his desert island'. These images suggest she provides him with comfort, sex and also refuge. The adjective  'beached' is significant too as it emphasises the woman's immobility, which is implicit in all the other images of herself. A 'beached' whale is out of its natural element, trapped, helpless and vulnerable. Without help a beached whale will probably die. Like this woman.

- Metaphorical references to her physical size give way to more direct rhetorical language, such as the repetition of 'too fat to...' The tone is difficult to determine here. Is the woman ashamed of her condition? Her voice sounds neutral, merely cataloguing events, emotionally detached from her own experience, perhaps even numb. Certainly, though the narration is retrospective, there is a noticeable absence of reflective commentary expressing her thoughts or feelings

- The power dynamic shifts between the characters: 'I allowed him to stroke' implies she has some control. And this raises a troubling aspect of the characterisation of the woman; her apparent compliance in her own abuse. In the next line, for instance, the man says 'Open wide' and he pours 'olive oil down' her 'throat'. The woman is either unable or unwilling to resist. Earlier she had said her 'only pleasure' was the 'rush of fast food' the man feeds her. The monstrous descriptions of her body also come from her own mouth

- The understated, matter of fact tone of the horrific last line: 'There was nothing else left eat' so casually explaining resorting to cannibalising his dead body confirms our sense of growing unease with the narrator as the poem progresses.

This last point takes us back to irony in dramatic monologues. Clearly there is an ironic gap here between what the character is saying and what the writer wants the reader to understand by it. She has in fact been turned into a monster by her abuser, but the question remains to what extent did she have some responsibility for the situation. The poem poses, but does not answer this ethical question.

3.

Why is the poem written in rhymes three line stanzas?

Technically three lined stanzas are called 'tercets'? The form reminds me a little of Dante's use of terza rima in *The Divine Comedy* and these gluttonous, dysfunctional characters could, perhaps, be found in a modern version of Dante's outer circles of hell. Agbabi's tercets don't feature the chain rhyme characteristic of terza rima and the rhyme pattern, like the metre, has a roughness & looseness about it. Partly the use of half-rhymes rather than full rhymes help generate a believable speaking voice - Browning masterfully uses full rhymes in *My Last Duchess*, but obscures them with caesuras, enjambment and other devices - but the sounds that don't quite fit together might also suggest the tension in the relationship. The three-line structure might also remind us that there are three characters in the poem, the unnamed woman and man and behind them the poet.

Though the poem lends itself to a Feminist reading, the imagery might also interest postcolonial critics. As well as reference to a desert island, bread fruit is mentioned which might suggest a master/ servant, coloniser/ colonised dynamic could be mapped on the man and women in the poem. This reading would suggest that in the end the colonised subject will eventually become too big for the coloniser and lead, therefore, to the latter's inevitable destruction.

Crunching

Crunching a poem is a quick and interesting way of reducing the text to its most significant words. Only one word is allowed per line of the poem. I recommend you have a go at completing this task on your own at first and then compare your crunching with your peers. Through discussion see if you can come to an agreed class crunched version. Then compare your version to mine. I'm not presenting mine as the single correct crunch, but you'd have to work hard to convince me that my choices are wrong...

Of course, the crunching process can be usefully repeated all the way down to the most important few words, or even a single word, in a poem. And it can be easily adapted: Crunching the best lines, or images, crunching through picking out all the nouns or adjectives or verbs, and so forth.

Eat Me crunched:
CAKE – LAYERS – WEIGHT – PINK – EAT – TOLD – WALK – BED – WOBBLE – LIKE – BIG – MASSES – JACUZZI – PLEASURE – FORBIDDEN – BREADFRUIT – WHALE – FLESH – FAT – SHIELD – TOO – ALLOWED – GLOBE – OPEN – WHISPERED – TOP – DROWNED – WEEK – GREED – EAT.

In Edexcel's AS exam students have to answer one out of a choice of two questions. Both questions require comparison of two poems. On each question one poem will be selected by the board; the choice of the matching poem will be left to the students:

e.g. Compare the ways in which poets explore the shift from childhood to adulthood in *An Easy Passage* and one other poem. In your answer you should consider:

- themes
- language & imagery
- the use of other poetic techniques

For *Eat Me* the question could ask about male and female relationships or the presentation of the female character. If that were the case, good comparison poems would be *The Gun*.

Simon Armitage: *Chainsaw Versus the Pampas Grass*

1.

What do you make of the title of Armitage's poem?

Firstly, it is intended to sound like a sports match or a fight. There's no article

('a' or 'the') at the start which also makes 'chainsaw' sound like a name of a person or a team. If we think of chainsaws and their place in popular culture for just a moment or two we'll soon hit on the notorious horror film *The Texas Chainsaw Massacre*. Chainsaws are serious bits of kit, powerful and dangerous tools that can be wielded as weapons by nutcases in horror films. Powerful and dangerous are not words we would usually associate with the rather flimsy, thin stemmed and fluffy headed pampas grass, as shown below, wafting gently in the wind.

Perhaps you've whiled away some time in a lesson or when waiting for a bus by playing imaginary match-ups. Which would win in a battle between a shark and a crocodile? Would a tiger defeat a lion? Who'd come out on top in a final showdown between Superman and Batman? Would Nigella Lawson take down Mary Berry? In this game the contestants have to be well matched, otherwise there's obviously no fun in the speculation and not much of a fight. In pitching a deadly weapon, armed with rotating sharp serrated teeth propelled by a powerful motor incongruously against some defenceless wavy grass, Armitage makes the battle seem comically one-sided, like Superman vs. Mary Berry. As the first line of the poem acknowledges, 'It seemed an unlikely match'. Inevitably the grass will be wiped out, quickly and easily. Or so we are encouraged to think.

Notice that the poem's speaker is not included in the title: It is not *Armitage & the Chainsaw versus the Pampas Grass*. This adds to the sense that the chainsaw is a distinct character in the poem, acting almost autonomously, with a will of its own. It also excuses the speaker from responsibility for the anticipated carnage to come.

If I were teaching this poem, before reading the poem at all, I'd take some of the lines describing the chainsaw and present these to the class and ask them to speculate about who or what is being described. The same exercise could be done with the phrases describing the pampas grass. A third list would indicate the role of the speaker and their feelings about what they're doing. Students could then try to imagine what would happen when these three agents are brought together in the poem. Alternatively, the class could be split into groups each given one of the following lists (obviously without the titles!):

The Contestants: 1. Chainsaw

Here are some of the key phrases used to personify Chainsaw an active agent in the poem's narrative:

- Grinding its teeth

- Knocked back a quarter-pint

- Lashing out at air

- Bloody desire

- Swung/ nose-down from a hook

- Instant rage

- Perfect disregard

- Sweet tooth/ for the flesh

- Its grand plan
- Gargle in its throat
- Rear up

- Flare
- The hundred beats per second drumming in its heart
- Seethed

The Contestants: 2. The pampas grass

- Ludicrous feathers
- Taking the warmth and light
- Stealing the show
- Dark, secret warmth
- Riding high
- Severed
- Mended

- Plumes
- Sunning itself
- Swooned
- Its nest
- Wearing a crown
- The fringe

The Contestants: 3. The poet speaker

The speaker may present themselves mainly as an observer in this comic epic battle, but, obviously, they are not neutral or passive, as the following verbs and phrases illustrate:

- Trailed
- Walked back
- Clipped them together
- I let it
- Felt
- Threw
- Dabbed
- Raked
- Looked on

- Fed it out
- Flicked the switch
- Dropped the safety catch
- Lifted
- Touched
- Poured
- Ripped
- Drove
- Left it

Pulling all the phrases describing the chainsaw together in this way should help to highlight how it is presented as a sort of murderous villain. In fact, the chainsaw is rather like Mr Hyde (pictured below) from Stevenson's Gothic novella, *The Strange Case of Dr Jekyll and Mr. Hyde*: Barely contained

 anger, held on a short fuse, is signalled by 'grinding its teeth' and by 'seethed'. Dynamic verbs suggest the capacity for sudden, frantic, dangerous action, 'knocked', 'swung', 'flare'. The last of these verbs, of course, also suggests fire. Like a horse, the chainsaw, out of control, might 'rear up'. Other words signal murderous, possibly cannibalistic appetite: a 'sweet tooth for the flesh', 'bloody desire'. A lust for violence is indicated, even for senseless, ineffectual, mindless violence: 'lashing out at air'. But this violence can be also directed; there is a malign intelligence at work, a 'grand plan' and a 'disregard', perhaps for law or morality. Crucially, the chainsaw also seems as much a danger to the man wielding it as it is to the pampas grass.

Thinking of Mr. Hyde might lead us in the direction of a psychoanalytic reading of the poem, i.e. that the Chainsaw embodies the poet's subconscious desires. The speaker of the poem inhabits, after all, two separate perspectives; that of the character who wielded the chainsaw and tried to torch the stump as well as the reflective one, looking back at the experience, wryly observing his own foolish actions. This double identity, as participant and observer, is reflected in the verbs above. One phrase, in particular, links the man to the chainsaw: Just as the power tool had 'lashed' out at air' later in the poem the speaker describes himself using the saw as ineffectually: (it was) 'like cutting at water or air with a knife'.

The man's entrance into the poem is delayed until the second stanza, as if he is playing second fiddle to the main character, the chainsaw. But, in the fourth and fifth stanzas, the emphasis shifts to his actions. Look, for instance, at the number of uses of the first-person pronoun here. The most disturbing action of the poem takes place in this stanza: The man 'lifted the fringe', 'carved' at and 'ripped into' the hidden centre of the plant, its 'dark, secret warmth'. Transgressive, excessively violent, penetrative action gives way to obsession as the man repeatedly 'cut and raked'. Then he wants to 'finish things off'. The double perspective of insider and outsider is apparent in the emotive language employed do describe both the man's action and its effect on the plant. In addition to the examples cited above, the cutting is presented as a beheading; he 'docked a couple of heads'. The man also seems to get carried away with his destructive power, to be enjoying it; 'this was a game'. Three emotive verbs 'severed', 'felled' and 'torn' are used in close proximity to describe what he does to the grass, all of which can be applied to human beings, especially to limbs severed and soldiers felled in battle.

2.

Opposites attract?

The poem is structured on antithesis and the pampas grass is presented as an opposite to the chainsaw. Whereas the details of the chainsaw cohere into a pretty definite, voracious and villainous image, the pampas grass is harder to imagine as a single character. The feathers, plumes and nest, for instance, suggest a bird, the theatrical showiness of which might make us think of a peacock. But there's something comical too, its feathers are 'ludicrous', and it 'swoons', something heroines used to do in black and white films. Perhaps there's something of the diva or an old-fashioned show girl too in its self-indulgence and greed for warmth and light. 'Riding high' and 'wearing a crown' could fit with this interpretation. Whereas the chainsaw is full of destructive intent, the grass is presented as if sun-bathing, as relaxed and blissfully unaware of the coming violent attack.

It is clear is that the conflict in Armitage's poem is between potent, active male forces (the man, the chainsaw) and a seemingly passive and fragile female force, embodied in the pampas grass. If you're not convinced of this gendered reading, look up the word, 'swoon'; most definitions stress that this verb describes an apparently uniquely female form of fainting brought on by the close presence of an attractive man! Golly!

As we have already emphasised this male vs. female/ man & machine vs. nature fight appears to a preposterous mismatch. However, despite all the violence inflicted on it by the man and the chainsaw, despite all the cutting and docking and slicing and carving and burning, after just a few weeks the pampas grass triumphantly mends, resurrects and re-grows itself:

Tips/ sprang up from its nest...wearing a new crown.

And, in contrast to this bursting, exuberant fertility, man and chainsaw are rendered passive, impotent and redundant.

Featuring a man in relation to nature, thematically Armitage's superficially comic narrative prose poem has something in common with Romantic poems such as Wordsworth's **Nutting** and Shelley's **Ozymandias**. In *Nutting* the young poet chances upon an untouched scene of natural beauty and then senselessly ravages it. In Shelley's poem a speaker happens upon the ruins of a statue of the mighty Pharaoh surrounded by a seemingly endless desert. On the pedestal of the statue are the words 'Look on my works, ye mighty, and despair', a self-
aggrandising statement that is immediately undercut by the statue's location where only 'the lone and level sands stretch far away'. In other words, the works of man are pitiful and puny when set against the immense power of nature and time. (For a detailed examination of Shelley's poem see **The Art of Poetry, volume 1.**)

In Armitage's poem, which I'd like to call Domestic Romantic, the field of conflict between man and nature has shrunk from a desert to a back garden, and man has now created powerful, destructive tools to help him in his fight to control nature. But the outcome is the same; time and mother nature defeat man and machine. This is the truth the reflective speaker of the poem realises and that, as a destructive agent in the poem, he had foolishly forgotten.

Crunching

The officially correct, utterly indisputable, absolutely unarguable version of Armitage's poem crunched is as follows:

MATCH – GRINDING – DARKROOM – HATCH – KNOCKED – JUICES – ACROSS – DRY – GULP – HEAT – WRECKAGE – SPIDER'S – I – GARDEN – POWDER – FLICKED – COUPLED – GUNNED – RAGE – LASHING – MOOD – TANGLE – BLOODY – FLESH – PLAN – REAR – FLARE – HEART – THROAT – FEATHERS – PLUMES – SUNNING – SHOW – SPEARS – SLEDGEHAMMER – NEED – LEVER – OVERKILL – EXIST – SWOONED – DISMISSED – GAME – CARVED – PLANT-JUICE – SECRET – WORK – SEVERED – DEAD – CUT – STUMP – EARTH – FINISH – DROVE – CHOKED – MENDED – KNIFE – POURED – MATCH – LEFT – NEW – SPRANG – CROWN – EGYPT – MOON – SEETHED – MAN-MADE – TIME – FORGET – PERSIST.

Agree entirely? Good.

Other poems that examine human interaction with nature include *The Gun*, *The Lammas Hireling*, *Giuseppe* and *History*.

Ros Barber: *Material*

1.

Look at Barber's poem on the page. <u>What strikes you about how it is</u> <u>arranged?</u> To me in looks very tidily regular and well ordered. Nine stanzas, each eight lines long, follow the same cross rhyme pattern, so that the second and fourth lines rhyme with each other. This pattern is then neatly mirrored in the second half of each stanza, so that the sixth and eighth lines also rhyme with each other. Many of the stanzas comprise one sentence and almost all finish at the end of a sentence with a definite full stop. Listen to the poem and you'll notice the metre is regular too; iambic tetrameter ticks away steadily throughout the poem with very few trips, hiccups or variations. A pleasantly neat sonic and syntactical effect is thus created and sustained from stanza to stanza, making each one sound rounded off, satisfyingly complete.

Examine the language of the poem (sometimes called the diction) and you'll find nothing shocking or badly behaved there either. There are no extravagant or fanciful metaphors or potent rhetorical devices, no exotic sound effects and few showy or erudite words ('lassitude' might perhaps be an exception). Nor do words smash together in explosive, original or surprising combinations to generate semantic fireworks. The poem's language does not draw attention to itself. Like its form and structure, it is exemplary in its well composed, unostentatious orderliness.

How do you feel about this trimness and tidiness? Is it to be admired for its craftsmanship? How might it relate to the poem's title and themes? Is all this repeating of strict patterns a little excessive, even oppressive, perhaps? We'll come back to that thought at the end of this essay.

Imagine a class of perfectly behaved, neatly dressed, quiet, biddable children. In this dream class is one child who is loud, scruffy and badly behaved. When there is so much that is so well ordered deviations to the norm tend to stick out. In Barber's poem there are just a few disruptive elements. For example,

 in the fifth stanza the second line end word 'foot' does not rhyme with its pair word 'butcher'. But that's a minor deviation. Compared to its polite peers,

Stanza six is almost a delinquent: Not only does it have an extra ninth line, thus throwing the rhyme scheme out of joint, but its second and fourth lines do not rhyme either! ('talons' & 'piano'). If that wasn't enough already, it's also composed of two sentences (mind you, so are about half of the stanzas, so that's not that rebellious). And, and, stanzas five & six are the only stanzas which share a sentence between them and are thus linked by enjambment.

Clearly there's something going on in the middle of this poem. <u>The question is what?</u>

A cynical student might suggest that the poet was just unable to keep the form going and couldn't think of a rhyme for 'talons' (though 'balance' quickly springs to mind in this context). Perhaps the cynic is right, but it's more productive to assume that writers are masters of their craft and as marked a deviation as an inclusion of an extra line quite deliberate. Broadly this is the middle section of the poem, the hinge point where attention will turn away from the mother and the lost world of which she was part to focus on what her daughter has inherited from her. Perhaps the losing of tight control on the  regular pattern foreshadows the daughter's difficulty in following her mother's fixed example. This section of the poem is also about loss of a once familiar and predictable world, of the local greengrocer whose name you knew and the friendly butcher and the Annual Talent Show. A little emotional wobble in the form seems therefore appropriate here.

The central image of the poem is a **metonym**: The old-fashioned handkerchief represents the mother and a whole way of life. Noticeably, the speaker's mother behaves in the same conventional, collective way as other women, waving hankies out of trains, using them to mop tears and whip away rouge, always prepared for emergencies with a hanky up her sleeve. In comparison, the narrator has not been able to follow the orderly and conventional pattern of behaviour set by her mother:

There's never a hanky up my sleeve.

And instead of watching her children perform, the speaker focuses on her own creativity, writing a poem, keeping her children happy by sticking them in front of the TV. Clearly she's not the mother her mother was. Guilt creeps in with 'I raised neglected-looking kids'. But the speaker rallies. Despite feeling sorrow and loss for the 'soft hidden history' the handkerchiefs embodied, she decides she can 'let it go' and her 'mother too, eventually', though, that small pause is, of course, telling. The poem ends with a witty pun leading back to the title:

This is your material
To do with, daughter, what you will.

As well as the physical material of the hanky, this refers, of course, to the material of her life which she can turn into writing material. Such witty touches are a feature of a poem that might be categorised as light verse. Indeed, with its lightly satirical social commentary and self-deprecating style, Barber's poem has something in common with the work of John Betjeman or a Movement poet, such as Philip Larkin, in his gentlest mode. Other examples of wittiness include the idea of there being so many hankies stuffed up sleeves ('as if she had a farm up there') that they must have fallen in love and mated to produce 'little squares'. Or the notion that male children were given larger handkerchiefs for Christmas because 'they had more snot'.

2.

A well-made poem

Radical avant-garde poets would probably be appalled by the idea that a poem could be constructed around as mundane a subject and written in such a neat, well-made form. But modern poets often pay special attention to the apparently small and insignificant. Barber uses a hanky as a gateway to writing about her mother, their relationship, her own sense of herself as a mother and of how society has changed, for better and worse, over time. Indeed, the poem argues that even small changes in behaviour can have major, large scale effects; the loss of the hanky triggers, eventually, the 'shuttered the doors of family stores'.

Back to the question we posed about whether the poem's pervasive tidiness.  To me, this seems a bridge between the poet and her mother. Though the poet's behaviour as a mother might have fallen short of the conventional example she was set, she is a match for her mother in the neat orderly arrangement of words on the page. Indeed, it's not too fanciful to suggest that those tidy stanzas visually look like little pocket squares. Total uniformity, however, would have been oppressive. Hence that deviant stanza six.

Crunch Time

QUEEN – HANKY – PAPER – GARAGES – WAVING – GRIEF – MATERIAL – SLEEVE – CARDI – LACE – EMBROIDERED – SPITTLED – OUT – FARM – LOVE – MATED – NEVER – PRESENTS – SETS – PONCE – NAFFEST – BROTHERS – MALE – SNOT – CLOSED – GIRDLES – HOMELY – MALLS – DEMANDED – BOILING – STORES – DIED – LOSS – GREEGROCER – CAN – HISTORY – EXTRA – FISHMONGER – YOLKS – CRABE – DANCING – TALONS – TAUGHT – PIANO – STEP – TALENT – FENCING – WHIP – SMUDGE – NOSTALGIA – INNOCENCE – TEN-BOB – KILLED – ME – BUY – EAT – COMMIT – NEVER – NEGLECTED – STRANGERS – FORBIDS – BAG – PACKS – MISS – HIDDEN – GO – EVENTUALLY – DIED – TISSUES – COMPLAIN – DISPOSABLE – MATERIAL – WILL.

With the relationship between mother and daughter at the heart of **_Material_**
this poem links with **_Genetics_**. A mother-child relationship is also central to
On Her Blindness and **_Out of the Bag_**.

John Burnside: *History*

1.

Doubles

There's a curious pattern in Burnside's poem that is so insistent in can only have happened by design. Right from the get-go many of the phrases are arranged in patterns of two: The sand and the smell of gasoline; the tide 'far out' and 'quail-gray'; the people 'jogging' or 'stopping to watch' and the planes; the planes that 'cambered and turned'. The pattern is there in the nouns - sand, smell, people, planes - as well as in the verbs or verb phrases as well as in the adjectives. Not convinced? Okay, now you've asked for it:

Nouns	Verbs	Adjectives
The news and the dread	The drift and tug	Captive and bright
The speaker and Lucas	Scarcely register,	Nerve and line
Shells and pebbles	scarcely apprehend	
Kinship or given states	Gazed upon and	
The world and our dreams	cherished	
The wind and the shore		
Gravity and light		
Distance and shapes		
Silts and tides		
Rose or petrol blue		
Jellyfish or anemone		
Light and weather		
Toddler and parent		

There that's proved it, I hope. And there will be more examples. Look, for instance, at the word 'Today'. Having established this insistent pattern of twoness we might then wonder at its signficance, particularly in relation to the poem's title. Before we do that, we'll just comment on another feature this systematic process foregrounds; how dominant nouns are in this poem, especially concrete ones. Action is comparatively scare - verbs are few on the ground and those present are reflective, not dynamic ones. This is a poem, then, composed of things – and those things are generally presented starkly, without the decoration or modification of adjectives.

Back to the significance of this pattern. As the relationship of the grand, abstract title to the specific concrete subtitle inidcates, this mediative, seemingly loosely structured poem sets small apparently insignificant details of personal history against the backgroup of world-changing global events, in particular the 9/11 terrorist attacks on the United States. The poem also has a double perspective; it is comprised of close observation of a particular place and all its distinct components, i.e. the poet's gaze is turned outwards. But it is composed too of philosophical reflection, in which the
poet makes his thinking the poem's subject. World wide and personal events, outer and inner experience, innocent childish and adult perspectives, Burnside's poem is constructed upon these antitheses.

2.

How does the poem's form relate to its theme?

The sense of movement created by the free verse form seems to embody the poet navigating his way between the binary poles of antitheses. He is navigating the space 'lost between the world we own/ and what we dream about'. The path is uncertain and he is unsure of his steps. Hence stanzaless lines shift about, starting and ending at different points. Some are very long and almost make it right the way across the page, others are much shorter;

the shortest is just one word of five letters. The poem is also metreless. So no underpinning pattern appears to regulate its movement. It's as if the ground under the poet's feet is unstable, shifting, uncertain.

Sometimes the lineation suggests the in and out movement of waves on a shore:

> **I knelt down in the sand**
> **with Lucas**
>   **gathering shells**
> **and pebbles**
>   **finding evidence of life in all this**
> **driftwork**

But even the irregularity isn't stable: At other times, when the poem moves inwards into explicit thinking and reflection, the lineation falls into a more regular pattern. Lines resolve into fixed, more solid stanzas, as in the lines starting with '**at times I think...**' and later on with '**Sometimes I am dizzy**'.

Sentence structure adds to the fluidity of the poem's form and the sense of potential disconnection and fragmentation. The first elongated sentence, with its multiple clauses and pile up of phrases, for example, does not come to the end of its weaving, winding journey and its full stop until over half a page and 21 lines later. Indeed the whole poem is composed of only three stretched-out sentences. Between the isolated adverb of time that begins it – 'today' - and the rest of the sentence this word modifies 'I knelt down in the sand' there are, for example, 13 lines. In between these the reiteration of the word, 'today', followed by another long pause of blankness, makes it seem as if literally no time has elapsed since the first line. Looseness, potential fragmentation, hesitation, silence, are generated too through the use of these blank spaces ably aided by the punctuation. Look, for instance, at the number of hyphens on the first page; there are two more of these uncertain, skittish marks here than there are full stops in the entire poem.

3. Seeking connections

Unsurprisingly, in all this local unfixedness and the global turmoil it mirrors, the poet seeks out images of forces that prevent things from drifting entirely apart, stuff which connects things together securely: The kites are emphatically 'plugged' into the sky; bodies are 'fixed and anchored'; water 'tethers' the people to gravity; the fish are 'lodged' in the tide. At other times the poet himself forges these connections, as in the lines:

Snail shells, shreds of razorfish;
Smudges of weed and flesh on tideworn stone,

Here a run of sonic devices, sibilance and assonance, enhanced by the way, syntactically the phrase 'and flesh' can be linked to smudges or to stone, re-enforces the shared lexical field. Diction and sounds lock together to form a whole.

The ordinary, seemingly stable world can seem suddenly more vulnerable and precious in the light of global disasters. Burnside's poem encourages us to value, connect to and find meaning in what is immediately around us, the

world we can touch and smell and hear and see and our relationships within it. Attend to the delicate, temporal 'shifts of light/ and weather' outside and inside ourselves, the poet suggests. He provides us with an enduring image of how to live in this world and 'do not harm' in the 'toddler', an innocent everyman figure, curious about the world around him. We are all, the poem, implies 'sifting wood and dried weed from the sand', 'puzzled by the pattern'. All we can hope is like another child, Lucas, we can find meaning, 'evidence of life' in 'all this driftwork'.

If that sounds like a conclusion, it was meant to. But it isn't. Burnside's poem doesn't in fact end with the lingering image of the child, but with the parents. Parents are figures of experience, more conscious of the wider world around them and Big Scale History surrounding their own histories. The final line of the poem is striking and unexpected because it ends with a single adjective 'irredeemable'. Why do you think Burnside choose this one word rather than a synonym such as 'irrevocable' or 'transitory' or over the two-word pattern we have seen so dominant throughout the poem? Clearly the poet wanted a word that carries the moral sense of sinful beyond salvation as well as the idea of being beyond cure or remedy. Recalling T.S.Elliot's use of 'unredeemable' about time in **Burnt Norton**, 'Irredeemable' also contains the sense of time that cannot be recovered. Hence packed into this single word the essential twoness of the poem, its two narratives of personal and global History are finally wielded together.

Crunch Time

I've already implied the poem can be crunched to a couple of key lines; the one about finding evidence of life in the driftwork and the final line. It's a long poem to crunch, so I'm going to miss out a few lines:

TODAY – WE – BEACH – SMELL – TIDE – PEOPLE – WAR – MORNING – TODAY – NEWS – KNELT – LUCAS – FATHERING – EVIDENCE – DRIFTWORK – STONE – THINK – KINSHIP – LOST – DREAM – RAISED – ANCHORED – CONFINED – TETHERS – WATER – READING – TIDES – ROSE – JELLYFISH – CHILD'S – FEAR – LOSING – LIVING – VIRTUAL – REGISTER – APPREHEND – MOMENT – LOCAL – LODGED – INSOMNIA – BRIGHT – HUNG – GOLD – HOME – HUM – PROBLEM – CHERISHED – TODDLER – SIFTING – PATTERN – PARENTS – PLUGGED – PATIENT – IRREDEMABLE.

A poem about identity and the interaction between the personal and public world, **History** could be compared with **To my Nine-Year-Old Self** and **Genetics.** Although it's not in the *Poems of the Decade* anthology, because it was written almost 150 years ago earlier, an interesting companion piece to Burnside's poem would be **Dover Beach** by Matthew Arnold. I don't think it's possible to write a 'beach' poem in English without being aware of this famous predecessor and, intertextually, Burnside's poem can be read as in dialogue with Arnold's. As well as an end of the land/ start of the sea setting, the poems share a similarly pensive mood and Arnold also uses form to suggest the movement of waves, backwards and forwards. <u>How, though are they different?</u> Arnold's poem laments the loss of the 'bright girdle' of religion biding the world together; <u>what does Burnside find that might take the place of this holding force?</u> Certainly, there is a spiritual, quasi-religious feel to Burnside's poem – the poet kneels in the poem, he mentions a 'book' of nature and he finishes with something like a creed, but, in the end, it's a way of thinking and being in the world that is offered as hope.

Julia Copus: *An Easy Passage*

1.

Halfway

Used in film and narrative studies, the term *in media res* describes an opening that throws the audience straight into the middle of the action already happening. Copus's unmetred, filmic free verse poem begins in this manner, midway through the story:

Once she is halfway up there

A character is mentioned, as if we have already been introduced to them, and a place, as if we know where 'there' is. The term *liminality* is used in literary studies to describe inbetween states, when things are neither quite one thing nor another. As they are neither night nor day, dawn and twilight, for instance,  are liminal states; similarly, neither dead nor alive, a vampire is a liminal Gothic figure. The fact that the poem starts halfway through and the girl is halfway up suggests Copus is interested in the space in between things and the transition from one state to another. The title of this enigmatic poem, which recalls the phrase 'rites of passage', allied to the fact that the central character is a teenage girl, in addition to the detail that she is 'half in love', added to the fact that she is suspended for most of the poem on the point of moving from the outside to the inside, strengthens this impression.

After the initial establishing of the girl's location, action in the poem is suspended in the manner of a filmic cliff hanger. Copus uses a number of techniques to stretch and hold the moment out and thus to generate tension:

- Our omniscient narrator takes us into the girl's thoughts, 'she knows that...she must keep'
- Use of the present tense means we are uncertain of the outcome – perhaps the girl will fall
- Reference is made to the danger and precariousness of her situation, 'the narrow windowsill' and 'sharp drop'
- Description of what she can see from her restricted and concentrated field of vision, 'the flimsy, hole-punched, aluminium lever'
- The first sentence runs for 13 lines, at the end of which she still hasn't actually entered the house: 'In a moment she will...' is in the future tense
- In the following sentences she is still held immobile. Tactile imagery helps us share her physical sensations, 'the asphalt/ hot beneath her toes'
- Authorial intrusion in the form of philosophical reflection slows time: 'What can she know/ of the way the world admits' taking us out of the time of the story into time of the mind
- Cross cuts to other characters: the mother, the factory workers, the secretary, the other girl, arrest the movement of the suspended girl's narrative.

Only in the last sentence of the poem does time start up again, the girl cross the threshold and drop into the house.

2.

The girls

Like icons in religious paintings, the two girls seem radiant, 'lit, as if form within' and are both associated with light, 'shimmering', 'flash'. They are also utterly absorbed in their experience, so that the house 'exists only for them'. Their near nakedness is emphasised by the reference to the 'bikini', to 'tiny breasts' and in the phrase 'next to nothing'. Conventionally nakedness would signify vulnerability, but, despite the precarious predicament, the girls do not seem weak. In fact, in the poem's final simile associates them with powerful explosive weapons: 'like the/ flash of armaments'. Accompanied by this momentous explosion, the girl crosses the threshold (into the house/ into adulthood) completes her passage from one state to another with ease and indeed, 'gracefully'.

3.

Other characters

There are two other female characters in the poem, the mother and the secretary. Both are described as 'far away' from the girls, as if they are in another dimension entirely, far away in experience as much as in space. The mother has not trusted her daughter with a 'key' to the house, which, if we take the act of breaking into the house as symbolising moving from girlhood to womanhood, implies the mother wishes to prevent her daughter from growing up. With her head full of distractions, the secretary seems to stand as an opposite to the girls. They are totally absorbed in the moment as it is happening, whereas the secretary is reading an 'astrology column' trying to find evidence of fate. Rather than acting as a determining agent in her own narrative she is waiting for things to happen to her.

The startling, surreal image of 'long grey eye of the street' suggests an audience or camera watching the girls, making tangible the filmic quality of the poem. The most important fact is that the girls can act unwatched by an outside eye, they are free from its potentially controlling gaze and from social mores. Freed, they can grow up.

The relationship between them

Like characters from a William Blake poem, the girls are presented as dynamic figures of innocence, contrasted starkly to the experienced perspective of the road's eye, the factory workers and the two other women. The central philosophical question in the poem which appears nearly in the poem's centre, 'What can she know/ of the way the world admits us less and less/ the more we grow', implies that as we get older we lose direct connection with our experience. Thinking about it, reflecting on it, planning alternatives and so forth, we stop feeling it in the present, now. Whereas when we were young, like these two girls, we felt experience more intensely, sensuously and directly, tasted it on our tongues.

4.

What, no stanzas?

Throwing light on the decisions the writer made, rearranging the form of a poem is always a potentially interesting exercise. What difference, if any, would it make if Julia Copus had written her poem in a neat series of quatrains, or in an irregular stanza form or, perhaps, in couplets? The fact that the poem is a single unbroken whole is certainly striking. Like a single, sustained, sweeping camera shot, this unbroken form implies that all the poem's content is part of one single picture, one interconnected situation; a whole, in fact. Only with the poem's last line, when everything is changed, will a new situation begin. This is such a major break, such a significant change, in fact, that the poem cannot continue. Indeed, if this poem were a novel, its final line would function like a chapter break. Imagining what happens next, we might be able to write the next poem. Perhaps this new poem could begin with, 'Dropping gracefully into the shade of the house'.

With an unmetred, unrhymed prose poem such as *An Easy Passage* the lineation is crucial. If lineation is not done well, a poem degenerates into prose chopped up, prose merely masquerading as verse. To test the effectiveness of Copus's lineation we should be able to take a few lines at random and examine their design. We might, for instance, consider the fourth to sixth lines. In the first of these the poet obviously wanted a gap between the words 'sharp' and 'drop' for mimetic effect. Rearrange the line, move 'drop' to line four and this effect is tangibly diluted. Similarly, the small pause after 'mind' in the next line makes us wonder, for a moment, what it is she must keep her mind on, taking us into the girl's experience. In the sixth line it is clear that Copus wanted the word 'love' to carry the emphasis achieved by placing it at the end of the line, so that the sentence and the lineation build toward this significant word.

In a similar vein, we might also examine Copus's use of breaks in the middle of lines, a device known technically as caesura. The most emphatic caesura concludes the first sentence of the poem not at the end, but within the line:

...to the warm flank of the house. But first she

Though the girl shares this line with the house, which is itself described here as if it were, like her, alive, she is also separated from its comforting 'warm flank' by the caesura. Hence closeness and distance, connection as well as separation are neatly re-enforced. Notice too how the break at 'she' leaves the girl hanging for a moment at the end of the line, the pronoun waiting for its connecting, reassuring verb, 'steadies'. If you're still not convinced that careful design has gone into the lineation in this poem try examining the rest of the lines to see if you can propose better points at which to start and end them.

The Crunch

HALFWAY – TREMBLING – MUST – NARROW – DROP – LOVE – WAITING – BENEATH – WINDOW - FLIMSY – MOMENT – LEANING – FLANK – CROUCHING – TOES – PETRIFIED – KNOW – LESS – GROW – LIT – EXISTS – ONLY – EYE – TRUST – DRAB – FACTORY – FAR – FULL – PLANS – OMENS – THIRTEEN – NOTHING – STOMACH – GAZE – SHIMMERING – OUTSTRETCHED – SUNLIGHT – ARMAMENTS – DROPPING.

With its Blakean theme of innocence and experience, **_An Easy Passage_** links to **_To my Nine-year-old self_**. The metaphorical journey connects it to **_The furthest distance I've travelled._**

Tishani Doshi: *The Deliverer*

1.

Think about the title for a moment. <u>What are the different connotations of the word 'deliverer'?</u> Clearly the subtitle gives the poem a religious setting and in this light 'deliverer' takes on the sense of Christ, redeemer and deliverer of mankind from evil and sin. The poem is also about childbirth and we talk about delivering a baby. Thirdly, there is Catholic sister in this hard-hitting, laconically expressed poem who rescues the young girl. Lastly, there is the figure of another rescuer, the American mother who saves a girl who might, or might not be, the narrator herself. It seems, at first, that in rescuing the girl the adopting mother is a Christ-like deliverer. However, as the poem develops a more complex and uncertain, blurry picture emerges.

The details in the first stanza are starkly brutal. This is a context in which to be dark skinned or female is a form of disability. And to be disabled is to be called that much harsher, more pejorative term 'crippled'. And in such an unforgiving environment unwanted children are 'abandoned' 'naked'. If this were not horrifying enough, one girl is buried up to her neck underground. This girl, it transpires, might, or might not be, our narrator.

Isolated, as if it signals a new beginning, the final line of the first section of the poem appears initially to offer a happy ending to this short, tragic story:

This is the one my mother will bring.

The choice of a star * as punctuation resonates with the religious setting and seems further evidence of a hopeful resolution.

'Bring' is odd, though. <u>Shouldn't it be 'take'?</u> Bring would imply movement to the convent not from it. In which case the second reference to 'my mother' is to a different mother than the first one. Things are already more complex than they first appeared. The first time we came across the word 'mother' in the opening line of the poem we naturally would have assumed that it refers the narrator's biological mother. But, in fact, it seems more likely that it pertains to the adopted mother who is visiting the convent. It would seem odd if this first second mother is also the mother in the American couple, waiting at the gates for their new adopted daughter, as they 'haven't seen or touched her yet'. The next use of 'mother' refers back to the birth mother who not only abandoned her child but 'tried to bury' her, which implies this was the child mentioned in the first section found by the dog. Hence, when we next come across the word two lines later, there is a further blurring of characters. The results is that it becomes all but impossible to distinguish one mother from another. We must assume now that this is the American mother who is crying. Unnerving uncertainly creeps in with the next line, 'feeling the strangeness of her empty arms'. We do not have a distinct, single subject; it could be the mother or the narrator who has this 'feeling' and why are the arms 'empty'? Due to the uncertain use of the word 'mother', is this perhaps a reference to the birth mother's loss? Added to this confusion of multiple possible mothers is the fact that the convent is named after another mother, **'Our Lady of the Light'.**

And who's to say the sister is telling the truth? She is 'telling' a story that

elicits sympathy, but <u>how do we know it is true?</u> It's quite possible in a complex context with a toxic mix of social shame, sin, child abandonment, poverty and adoption into a completely different culture, and nationality, that this is a convenient narrative hiding a more disturbing reality. Uncertainty is inherent at the start of the girl's life; she only has the story the sister tells to depend on.

Certainly, the third section of the poem suggests the transition into a new life was not as easy as the arrival at the airport seemed to promise. Growing up on 'video tapes' implies a virtual and westernised way of life. Distance from real life is repeated in the choice of the distancing three-person voice, if we assume she is writing about herself. If the poet is writing about another girl, then the fact that she remains anonymous 'the girl', creates a similar effect. Worse, the life's also unsettled. The child is 'passed from woman/ to woman'. Notice how the maternal link is also lost; she is not passed from one mother to another mother. Though she has moved into a different life, her personal history exerts a powerful pull on her imagination, implying that she cannot escape the past. Trying to return to her origins, as if there she might discover her true self, is a forlorn exercise. And, instead, of finishing optimistically, the poem ends with grim images of infanticide, a 'heap' of abandoned girl babies. It is as if this original trauma cannot be escaped or left behind. In this way, the poem explores the vexed issue of inter-racial, cross-cultural and inter-national adoption, as well as the complex ways we form a sense of our personal identities.

Postcolonial critics might be especially interested in this poem, with its seemingly stark contrast between two worlds. On the one side we have the apparently benevolent Catholic nuns saving children from terrible fates. The American couple too, who know 'about doing things right' who, from their perspective are also deliverers, are presented on this side of virtue. On other side we have a picture of life in India that is irredeemably brutal and bleak.

Crunch Time

MOTHER – CHILDREN – CRIPPLED – NAKED – GARBAGE – ABANDONED – DOG – POKING – CHEW – MOTHER – PARENTS – AMERICAN –RIGHT – TOUCHED – FETISH – BURY – CRYING – MOTHER – EMPTY – GROWS – PASSED – TWILIGHT – BIRTH – DESOLATE – OUTSIDE – LIFE – PENIS – HEAP – AGAIN.

With its focus on female experience and the complexity of identity *The Deliverer* could be linked to *An Easy Passage* and *Giuseppe*. Its concern with what we inherit from the past and this shapes our sense of ourselves also connects it to *Genetics*.

Ian Duhig: *The Lammas Hireling*

1.

This mysterious, supernatural narrative poem lends itself to translation into a film. Have a go at storyboarding your own version. Decide on a suitable setting, soundtrack, comprising music and ambient sound, as well as lighting, camera angles and so forth. Once you've completed this task you might want to compare with the following version: https://vimeo.com/45341598

Notice how swiftly the narrative moves through time in the first stanza. We go from the opening 'after the fair' to the magical effect the stranger has on the cattle in two short sentences and just four lines. The sensual simile 'fat as cream' recalls the phrase the 'cream of the crop', signalling the enriching influence of the hireling. <u>What is the effect of beginning the sentence 'then one night' at the end of the first stanza?</u> The caesura in the last line emphasises a distinct break, a sudden change in the relationship between narrator and the stranger. Enjambment facilitates smooth transition from the first to the second stanza and allows Duhig to place the word 'disturbed' in a prominent position at the start of the first line of the second stanza. Hence tension in the poem ratchets up quickly.

2.

A torn voice

The striking image of the wife's 'torn voice' uncannily distorts sound into something physical, tangible. Torn also suggests emotional suffering, loss but also perhaps violence. For some reason we cannot fathom, this hireling has taken on the voice of the dead wife and tormented the speaker out of his dreams with it. Or perhaps it is the farmer who projects his feelings onto what he hears. In any case, a filmic freeze frame then holds the narrative in suspense for a moment:

Stock-still in the light from the dark lantern,
Stark naked but for the one bloody boot of fox-trap

There is a growing sense of mystery and of the uncanny. The physical world is not operating in the ways we expect: paradoxically the lantern is 'dark', yet, light emanates from it. Has the mysterious stranger adopted the wife's voice because he has been caught in the fox-trap? Such a reading would seem to fit with 'torn'. Or is this what the narrator imagines? Why is he naked? Perhaps, he is shapeshifter, like a werewolf or other magical creature, that divests itself of the cloak of human clothing at night to resume its natural form. Nakedness also suggests vulnerability. Moreover, the hireling seems to be immobile. Is he a threat? Though the narrative has moved fast, we are now held in this prolonged moment of description - we do not know how the narrative will progress. The speaker might, for instance, feel sympathy. Is there something semi-erotic too in this scene? The stranger has taken the place of the wife as the narrator's companion in his home, brought fertility with him, takes on her voice, and now stands naked and helpless in the middle of the night.

But, then, unlike the reader, the speaker becomes certain: 'I knew him for a warlock'. The phrase 'to go into the hare gets you muckle sorrow' confirms the idea that the stranger is a shapeshifter, has turned himself into a hare and then been caught in a fox-trap. Or, at least, it confirms that this is what the poem's speaker believes. The proverbial sound of the phrase and the use of the Northern or Scottish dialect adjective, 'muckle' (very much) makes it sound like it is derived from inherited folk wisdom. It's as if this sort of thing – a man metamorphosing or being metamorphosed into a hare and then getting into some sort of fatal trouble – is not that out of the ordinary. We're in a strange, uncertain world in this poem.

Like his mind, the speaker's actions are decisive and definite. Despite all that it has done to bring him good fortune and makes his cattle fertile, as if appalled by the notion that the hireling has somehow taken on the role of his wife, he shoots him straight 'through his heart'.

 As with the voice being 'torn', abstract and concrete become uncannily mixed; it is time, the 'small hour' that the speaker fires. In addition to the strange interplay of light and dark, the reference to disturbing dreams and to a shapeshifting 'warlock', another Gothic trope, the moon, is introduced. The appearance of the moon often prefigures transformation in Gothic literature; think, for example, of a werewolf. In this transformation the hireling seems to return to his natural state, developing 'fur', 'like a stone mossing'. This gentle, natural image of metamorphosis is followed by surprisingly tender language. The hireling's head is described as 'lovely' and in another startlingly original visual image, his eyes 'rose like bread'.

3.

Transgressions

The poem's form continues to contribute to the unsettling, fatally transgressive atmosphere. Though the poem is composed in four even and orderly looking sestets, lines start and end in unusual places; in the middle of lines, at the end of them, overlapping from stanza to stanza. It's as if the sturdy form of the poem has been shaken, gone askew, disturbed like the narrator and his dreams. So, the narrative moves on and, at the end of the third stanza, the stranger's body is put in sack which magically grows lighter and by the next stanza it has been dropped off a bridge. So uncanny have the actions been so far that it almost doesn't come as a surprise to read that the dropped sack makes no 'splash'. These final details suggest that, perhaps, the hireling was a figment of the speaker's imagination, or that, at least, the scene in which the speaker shot him was. With its eerie transformation, perhaps the scene late in the house was actually a part of the farmer's dream.

Like the killing of the albatross in Samuel Taylor Coleridge's *The Rime of the Ancient Mariner*, the murder of the mysterious, fortune-bringing stranger brings a curse down on the narrator. He cannot even dream now of his dead

wife, and his herd, that was as 'fat as cream', is now afflicted by malign magic, 'elf-shot'. In another surprising development, the poem ends with the speaker using traditional Christian, specifically Catholic, language to try to absolve himself. The fact that it has only been 'an hour' since his 'last confession' may convey obsessive feelings of guilt or his desperation to find some way to mend his cursed fortunes. Or both.

Duhig's poem is a strange, beguiling, Gothic folk tale. The poet leaves the significance of the story for the reader to try to puzzle out. It is like a parable, but one whose meaning is not accessible to outsiders. Perhaps it is a sort of cautionary tale, warning us about how we treat the things in nature we do not understand and the harm we may do ourselves as a consequence of our ignorance. When confronted by the stranger's mysterious behaviour the speaker immediately demonises what he doesn't understand, precipitately jumping to the conclusion that the stranger is a 'warlock'. The title uses the Northern word 'lammas' which is connected to a pagan festival celebrating the wheat harvest. The mysterious stranger takes on the form of a hare, a conventional symbol of fertility. Perhaps then, he is a god of fertility, akin to the Greek God **Dionysus**, a character from myth presenting himself to a host in humble attire, whose transformational magic is misunderstood by the superstitious narrator and killed with his modern man-made weapon, a gun. After all, did this speaker really have to shoot the stranger, who had brought nothing but benefit into his life? You'll have to answer these questions yourself.

What is certain, I think, is that Duhig's poem is wonderfully rich and vivid, it weaves a magic like a charm itself. It is full of memorable images. The American poet Wallace Steven's dictum that '**The poem must resist the intelligence almost successfully**'. It is a great example of what the poet and critic Glynn Maxwell refers to as a 'lunar' poem in his useful book **On Poetry**; a poem that does not give up its meanings easily, but lingers in the mind after reading and haunts the imagination.

The Crunch

HEART – CHEAP – DOTED – CREAM – DOUBLED – NIGHT – DISTURBED – DARK – NAKED – WARLOCK – HARE – WISDOM - HEART – MOON – FUR – LOVELY – BREAD – SACK – DROPPED – ELF-SHOT – CASTING – BLESS – CONFESSION.

Featuring the entrance of something from another dimension into the ordinary world, Duhig's poem could be compared with **The Gun** and to **Giuseppe**.

Man's interaction with the nature links it to ***Chainsaw versus the Pampas Grass*** and with its mythical narrative mode and transformation scene <u>***The Lammas Hireling***</u> could be compared to ***Out of the Bag***.

Helen Dummore: *To My Nine Year Old Self*

1.

Imagine you're going to write a letter to yourself, from the distant future. Imagine you're in your sixties or seventies or even older. What would you write to yourself? What would you tell you about how your life has turned out? What advice might you give yourself about how best to face life's vicissitudes? Or, if that doesn't appeal, find a photo or small piece of film of yourself aged about five, about the age you would have started school, and write a piece to your younger self, updating yourself on how your life's turning out.

If you do have a go at either letter try to write freely, don't overthink it, just let whatever comes out flow as much as possible. Set yourself the challenge to write continuously for about fifteen minutes. Then try turning your text into a poem. Think of the transformation as a process of distilling or boiling down to absolute essentials. Choose only your best lines. Cut anything and everything you can, without losing sense. Think of yourself as Genghis Khan when you're doing this; be ruthless, cull, hack, obliterate, take no prisoners. Try to create a few holes in the story for the reader's  imagination to fill, make them work things out a bit. Then step back from the butchery, clear away the blood and see what you've got.

As teachers know too all well, there's a danger that once students start A-level English creative writing gets put on a back seat or is sent entirely to Coventry. A narrowing of the type of written responses to literary texts often takes place at this level, with the formal academic essay dominating. Some specifications offer the opportunity for students to try their hand at re-creative writing, which is always a challenging, but fun way of getting inside a text.

Taking on the role of the writer, deciding which way to go, choosing what language and devices to use, just keeping the engine of a text ticking over is demanding, akin to climbing into the driving seat of a racing car. And, nearly as exhilarating, maybe. And, however insightful the teaching, encountering every poem in this anthology through the same process of analytical reading would be reductive. Seek out and promote opportunities for creative writing; improving their creative writing will sharpen students' appreciation of writing craft and virtuously cycle back into the rest of the writing they do at A-level. It will also make palpable for them the fact that creative writing is a form of discovery, a way of thinking and of processing our life experience.

In her poignant, reflective and stylistically understated poem, Dunmore, a successful and acclaimed novelist for adults and children, creates a strong sense of her two characters and of the relationship between them. Starting her poem with the second person 'pronoun' she engages the reader in the relationship, placing us in the shoes of a silent addressee; hence we are aligned to the child. The short, stark first line immediately makes us wonder what the narrator must have done. So, straight-off, with minimum fuss Dunmore engages us in the world of the poem.

2.

The nine-year old Dunmore

What are the key characteristics of this silence listener?

Keen to be on the move, she is a fizz of boundless, dynamic energy. She embraces the experiences the world has to offer, revels in the freedom to simply express herself physically. Full of plans, she is interested in anything and everything, easily distracted, creative, entrepreneurial, fearless, vibrant, adventurous - an ebullient explorer of a world that seems new:

(she'd) **Rather leap from a height than anything...**
Jump straight out...into the summer morning

Even the darkness of life is faced down with bracing brio: It is the lanes that are 'scared' of men in cars and, having raised this spectre, the poem does not linger over it; enjambment ensures breezy onwards movement to another danger embraced with characteristic enthusiasm:

To lunge out over the water

All these images present the girl alone. The final image depicts her utterly absorbed in 'peeling a ripe scab', savouring the painful sensation and then the sensual experience of tasting it on her tongue. The image vividly captures her uninhibited fascination with experience, her complete, individual self-sufficiency, her freedom from social mores.

3.
Her adult self

The poem is, of course, constructed around a central antithesis. The narrator

presents herself, self-deprecatingly, as the opposite to her youthful self. A writer's life can be rather sedentary. Whereas her young self is characterised by dynamic verbs, 'run', 'climb', 'leap', 'lunge' and so forth, the older self's verb express regretful feelings, not movement: 'I have spoiled', 'I'd like to say', 'I have fears', 'I leave you'. Even the verbs need ancillaries. The adult self is full of sorrow and remorse, seeking forgiveness for having 'spoiled' her body. Carefreeness is replaced by having to move 'careful of a bad back'; fearlessness by having 'fears enough for us both'. In fact, the speaker ruefully admits that her two selves 'have nothing in common'.

The unmetred, unrhymed prose-like form of the poem, coupled with its lack of figurative or showy poetic techniques - figurative language is noticeable by its absence - make it seem direct, unguarded and honest. Our attention is directed not to poetic pyrotechnics, but to the speaking voice and is concentrated on the poignant relationship. The subtle sense of building up and dying away in the stanza pattern leaves the reader with a haunting sense of loss.

Crunch Time

MUST – GONE – TIGHTROPE – CLIMB – ANYTHING – SPOILED – SCARS – CAREFUL – REMEMBER – JUMP – MORNING – DREAM – WHITE – START – VOLE – AMBITION – ICE-LOLLY – DEN – LIKE – TRUTH – SHARED – TUPPENCE – HIDE – MEN – LUNGE – ROPE – BURIED – CLOUD – FEARS – ECSTASY – RIPE – TONGUE.

With its Blakean theme of innocence and experience and use of antithesis as a central structural element, *To My Nine-Year-Old Self* links to *An Easy Passage*. Its portrait of selfhood also links it to *Genetics* while *Out of the Bag* is also about childhood and growing up.

U. A. Fanthorpe: *A Minor Role*

1.

In the centre of the picture above are the central characters from Sophocles' Greek Tragedy, **Oedipus the King**, the protagonist, Oedipus, and his mother and wife, Jocasta. If U. A. Fanthorpe were in this picture she'd probably be the silhouetted figure at the back left. Fanthorpe's poignant, stoical poem celebrates the quiet heroism of unglamorous, but essential secondary roles and the sort of people who modestly, unostentatiously, uncomplainingly perform them.

Think of a hero or heroine and what sort of images spring readily to mind? The world of Hollywood seems at present to be dominated by muscle-bound, super-powered, super heroes - beings who are stronger, faster, just, well all round better, than mere mortals. Fanthorpe's poem offers a different type of quiet, selfless heroism.

2.

Slipping into the background

Like *Gallipoli, A Minor Role* is a list poem, busily full of ordinary, everyday verbs. Seemingly the poet herself, its protagonist is described as 'propping', 'making', 'driving', 'parking', 'holding', 'making sense of', 'asking', 'checking', 'getting on', and 'sustaining'. Repetition of all these present continuous tense verbs conveys the sense of endless and unending, mundane, but essential, chores. Syntax reinforces this impression. Look, for instance, at the last six lines of the second stanza: Each sentence fragment follows a very similar pattern. Notice too how the grammatically incomplete sentence, starting with 'Holding hands under/ veteran magazines' ending at 'civility', lacks one thing, a subject, the speaker who performs all these unherculean tasks. It's another way in which the poem's narrator slips easily into the background, even in her own poem.

Repetition occurs too across stanzas: Relocated from the hospital to the home, the second half of the third stanza follows a similar pattern to the previous stanza. Again, we have a list of actions, the terms of which are again separated by neat semi-colons; again, each item in the list starts with a verb, again in the present tense: 'answer'; 'contrive', 'find'. This sequence ends with a quickening flurry, as if the pressure is increasing: 'cancel', 'tidy', pretend', 'admit'. Of course, these last two verbs contradict each other; the impression of everything being under control is just that, an impression, an act. Underneath the appearance of coping, the narrator is, in reality, struggling to deal with a very traumatic situation. Even when a major break in the narrative is signalled by the use of three stars, the next stanza begins mid-sentence and immediately with another present continuous verb, one that evinces continual struggle, 'enduring'. All the while the poem's hard-pressed, industrious narrator is uncomplaining. Maintaining her composure and good manners, she asks questions 'politely', is 'grateful always', sustains 'the background music of civility', says 'thank you/ for anything to everyone'. Hence the reader is encouraged to feel sympathy and respect for this quiet form of domestic heroism.

Combining together a number of features generate the poem's briskness:

- a preponderance of verbs
- truncated sentences
- the listing pattern
- repetitive syntax
- a pervasive use of enjambment.

It's as if the narrator relentlessly presses on in order to suppress any feelings of self-pity that might otherwise surface. And, as the poem's title and opening allusion to acting indicate, the narrator is also aware of the pressure to keep up appearances, to play their part well. In other words, the poem's breeziness embodies the stoical attitude the narrator strikes for society. In poetic form, it is the analogue of the 'formula' the speaker adopts to ward off 'well-meant intrusiveness'.

That the situation really is difficult and traumatic becomes explicit in fourth stanza. Here the subtle linguistic metaphor of conjugation recalls all the previous verbs in the poem, all the stuff with which the narrator has had to cope. Conjugating 'all the genres of misery' suggests experiencing lots of suffering, 'tears, torpor' and so forth, but also a method for dealing with it. Working in combination with the literary metaphor of 'genres', the verb 'conjugate' implies a certain emotional distance on the experience, an ability to pull back and observe, or read it. To conjugate a verb implies understanding and control. Indeed, it may make us wonder, if we haven't already, whether the narrator is referring to her own misery or to someone else's.

The speaker in this poem is so self-effacing that it is not clear whether she is the ill party taking herself off to hospital and then caring for herself back at home. If she is speaking about her own illness, the distance between the busy narrative voice and the experiences depicted would signal the narrator's ability to step outside her own experience, observe and hence manage it. But perhaps, there is another silent, unnamed character in the poem, someone the speaker is actually looking after. In this second reading the 'hunger-striker' for whom the narrator is preparing meals is not herself, but her partner.

3.

Which do you think would make a more convincing interpretation?

To me, the second of these two readings is more credible. The poem's speaker tells us that habitually she takes a secondary, ancillary role. With her 'servant's patter' she does not take what she calls the 'star part'; she maintains the 'background music'. In the poem's narrative the main protagonist, the starring part, is surely the ill person; most of the action

revolves around their illness. And there definitely is another character in the poem. In the hospital the narrator is 'holding hands' with someone. The care and attention with which the narrator checks 'dosages' and 'dates', asks questions, plus the fact that she does the driving and parking suggests it is a partner who is ill. The references to telling people things are 'getting better', making meals for a 'hunger striker' and wanting a 'simpler illness' could, perhaps, be read either way. It seems more probable, however, that the cook and the hunger-striker are, in fact, two different people; that the narrator as carer is trying to make her ill partner eat.

If we read the poem as being about the partner's illness, not the narrator's, the last line also becomes freighted with greater urgency and emotional resonance:

I am here to make you believe in life

The 'you' in this reading is made more intimate and personal. This pronoun refers to us, the readers, of course, but also to an ailing beloved, silently present, listening in. The two readings subtly affect the tone of the line too: Addressed just to the reader, the tone is declarative and defiant; addressed to a beloved the line takes on an undertone, becoming almost a plea. Again extra poignancy is added. So, while both readings are valid, I'm inclined to favour the idea that this Fanthorpe's poem is about a relationship. Whichever way we read the poem, in the end, though, it is the narrator's heroic stoicism that comes through most strongly.

4.

Free verse

Fanthorpe's poem does not rhyme, nor is there a regular metre. The stanzas are also irregular - the last one just one line long. And yet, on the page, the poem looks fairly orderly. Clearly there is a sense in which the poem's form enacts the narrator's experience: Difficult, destabilising, emotional experience is wrestled into some sort of control – into words and sentences and stanzas - but is not contained by a reliable, predictable external pattern, such as a set poetic form. We have already mentioned the preponderance of enjambment; caesurae are used as frequently. Many of the poem's sentences start in the middle of lines, run over line ends, becoming long, winding lists. It is as if the stable form of the poem has been knocked slightly awry; order here is under intense pressure from forces of disorder. Though lines run over each other, each stanza finishes with an emphatic full stop. Like the narrator, the form of the poem may be subject to intense external strain, but it is holding fast, holding on. Just about. Or so it appears from the outside.

A few times prominent spaces are left between lines:

1. **For well-meant intrusiveness.**

    At home,

2. **For anything to everyone**

    Not the star part.

What might this striking typography convey?
In the first example, a significant separation is implied between the other people and the narrator. A sense of isolation is emphasised by the words 'at home' being stuck at the end of the line, preceded by emptiness and silence.

In the plays of Shakespeare and Harold Pinter, silences invite the audience to fill in a character's unspoken thoughts. In the second example, the implication of the first lines are left to linger for a while and, as with the first example, the most important words are emphasised by having a line to themselves, not at the prominent start however, but shunted to the back.

Expressed in an unshowy, 'unobtrusive', modest kind of language, Fanthorpe's poem is, as we have said, about a modest kind of heroism. But there's intellectual sophistication and steel underneath the self-effacing exterior. It takes courage to reject the wisdom handed down by great works of  literature. Fanthorpe quotes from the chorus on *Oedipus Rex* only to reject its sentiment emphatically: 'No it wouldn't'. Though the poem is full of ordinary everyday chores, the poet makes clear that these activities are not futile or inconsequential. In a poem composed mostly of literal language, Fanthorpe employs metaphors to ensure that these moments stand out:

- the 'monstrous fabric' of a play depends on the 'midget moments' being performed correctly
- the poet's actions at the hospital sustain, 'the background music of civility'

A reader might conclude that the poem's title should, in fact, be read ironically. What more major role can anyone play than making us believe in life?

Crunch Time

STAGE – ENDLESS – SERVANT'S – SIR – MONSTROUS – SHRINKS – UNOBTRUSIVE – ROLES – HOLDING – SENSE – ASKING – CHECKING – DATES – BACKGROUND – HOME – FAST – FORMULA – INTRUSIVENESS – HOME – BED – SOLVES – WARY – HUNGER-

STRIKER – HAPPY – REASSURING – PRETEND – ADMIT – MISERY – TEARS – SIMPLER – ENDURING – THANK – EVERYONE – STAR – WANT – TERRIBLE – ILL-ADVISED – DIE – BELIEVE.

Dealing with coping with suffering and relationships (with the self or with a partner), concerned with identity, *A Minor Role* could be linked to *Inheritance*. The traumatic nature of the experiences depicted in the poem could link it too to *Effects* and *On her Blindness*.

Vicki Feaver: *The Gun*

1.

What thoughts spring to mind when you read the first couple of lines of this poem?

Bringing a gun into a house
Changes it.

A home is a place of safety. Imagine a gun brought into your own house. How would your family react? What possible reason could there be for its arrival? How would it change the atmosphere?

Immediately in these two lines the poet establishes a sense of tension and danger. Notice how the poet uses space to generate suspense:

• A mini-space is left between the first line and the second. Feaver could just as easily have written the sentence as one line, not two. Which option is more effective? Why?

• These two lines are isolated from the body of the poem - another brief space for us to contemplate the lines' significance

• The poet doesn't give too much away; we know the gun changes things, but she doesn't tell us how, another space for our speculation to fill

• A fourth uncertain semantic space is created by the non-specific pronoun 'it', which can refer to the gun or the house. For now, the resolution of meaning remains suspended.

We are then introduced to a second person, the poem's auditor, 'you' who has brought in the gun. Unhurried lines convey unhurried action. The poem's paradoxical theme is subtly suggested: The gun is itself 'like something dead'. In the last four lines of this stanza there is a tightening of syntax and attention: Shorter lines contain a series of concentrated still images, one per line. Ominous details signal the gun's potential danger: 'jutting over the edge', for example, implies transgression, the crossing boundaries. The phrase 'Over the edge' implies losing control. The poet increases the foreshadowing – a 'shadow', for instance, is a common poetic metaphor for a ghost.

The tone changes with the casual sounding, looser, more conversational, 'At first it's just practice'. But this stanza moves swiftly - suddenly from harmless shooting of inanimate objects to killing a rabbit by shooting it through the head. The level of violence escalates unnervingly fast. In this light, 'at first' becomes more ominous; if this is what happens 'at first' what might happen, we wonder, 'at last'? The word 'shadow' hovers in the poem's tense atmosphere.

2.

Freedom

Feaver's poem is in free verse. No metre or rhyme scheme determines either line or stanza length. Or, indeed, the overall length of the poem. This structural looseness means the lines in the poem are hard to predict – they are not following a predetermined pattern which the ear and the eye can anticipate. <u>What stops free verse poems being prose randomly arranged into something just looking like verse?</u>

Firstly, the stanzas themselves; some principle must structure them. As we have already noted, in **The Gun**, for instance, there is clear design in the isolation of the first two lines. Subsequent stanzas outline the stages of a narrative. In the second, the gun is brought into the kitchen; in the third is put to use; the fourth stanza outlines the results of the gun's use; an isolated line follows, echoing, but modulating, the opening and the poem concludes with how the poet/ the poet's persona reacts. Secondly, lineation, the choice of where to start and end lines, is particularly important in free verse. A good rule of thumb is to assume the poet has put careful thought into this element of structure. Try re-arranging the lines, as we did with the opening two, to highlight the effects of the poet's choices. If the lineation is not purposeful then we do indeed have prose chopped up and dressing itself up as poetry. The middle lines from Feaver's fourth stanza illustrate her precise lineation:

Your hands reek of gun oil
And entrails.

Four elements of arrangement come together here to generate impact:
• the choice of syntax, so that the most important aspect comes at the end of the sentence

81

• a small delay, created by cutting the line before 'and entrails'

• the placing of this phrase at the start of the next line

• the caesura after 'and entrails', allowing its full effect to sink in. And linger.

Compare, for instance, an alternative arrangement:

Your hands reek of entrails and gun oil.

Here we have exactly the same words and broadly the same meaning, but all the tension, the shock impact of 'and entrails' has been lost.

The central theme of the poem, that closeness to death and killing paradoxically makes us feel more alive, is made more explicit at the end of the fourth stanza. The 'you' character is rejuvenated; they feel more alive, more youthful, more energetic: 'There's a spring/ in your step/ your eyes gleam/ like when sex was fresh'. The language of the poem is also invigorated here; sibilance, a stronger, more emphatic rhythm and running assonance combine to put a spring in the poem's quickening stride. In fact, the rhythm becomes almost a regular anapaestic one:

There's a **spring**
De de DUM

In your **step**, your eyes **gleam**
De de DUM, de de DUM

Like when **sex** was **fresh**
De de DUM de DUM

Here the close semantic connection between the words 'carnivore' and 'carnal' spring to mind. Resumption of the role of hunter has wakened other powerful, sensual appetites. After this quickening, there is a pause. And then Feaver delivers the long delayed information about exactly how the house has been changed:

A gun brings a house alive.

<u>What's surprising about this line?</u> Clearly as the gun is a bringer of death it's paradoxical that it can bring something back to life, like a miracle cure. Tonally too, the line's surprising. Up until this line the attitude of the poem's speaker to the introduction of the gun has remained tensely uncertain. Now, it seems, despite the gruesome entrails and the heap of dead animals. the speaker is not appalled, as we might have suspected; rather they too are excited, caught up in the increased intensity that the gun has  brought to the couple's life. To say the least, this is not a stereotypically female response to violence, bloodshed and the piling up of carcasses.

3.
The King of Death
The final stanza sees the speaker take their full part in the bloody enterprise. There is no squeamishness; like their partner, they are 'excited' as they perform a series of transformative actions which swiftly turn bloody carcass into meal. The poem ends with an extraordinary simile that relocates the action into some sort of mythical or fairy tale dimension. The figure of 'The King of Death' suggests both the Greek God Hades and the Grim Reaper, but

is, I think, Feaver's own invention. The medieval, fairy tale flavour of 'King of Death' is enhanced by the reference to his arrival 'to feast' from the 'winter woods'. It is as if the awesome figure of the 'King of Death' has been released into their dimension by the couple's return to hunting their meat – a huntsman, of course, is a key character in fairy tales. Out of his ominously 'black mouth' are sprouting 'golden crocuses'. Here the central paradoxical idea of the poem - that more intense life comes from closeness to death - is made concrete in a brilliantly visual, evocative image. Out of death's mouth new flowers blossom; beautiful and precious flowers - they are 'golden'.

According to Oxford Journals online the crocus species 'in spring are a symbol of the awakening of nature, of resurrection, even of heavenly bliss'. Saffron is produced from crocuses and, in classical literature, is the colour of the robe worn by the dawn and by Hymen, god of weddings. Both these associations fit with the idea of a new bright beginning, emanating from death.

Crunch Time
The poem crunched:

HOUSE - CHANGES – KITCHEN – DEAD – WOOD – JUTTING – BARREL – SHADOW – GREEN – JUST – TINS – ORANGE – GARDEN – RABBIT – HEAD – CREATURES – RUN – REEK – ENTRAILS – SPRING – GLEAM – SEX – ALIVE – JOIN – SLICING – DEATH – FEAST – WOODS – BLACK – CROCUSES.

For *The Gun* the question could ask about male and female relationships or the concentration on the effect of one object. Good comparison poems include *On her Blindness, Chainsaw* and *Eat Me*. *The Lammas Hireling* also explores the effect of a new element entering the domestic space.

Leontia Flynn, *The Furthest Distance I've Travelled*

1.

Defamilarisation

A hundred years ago Russian Formalist critics developed the theory of *ostranenie,* or defamiliarisation as it is known in English. These critics argued that in the modern age human responses become automated, deadened and unresponsive to the overly familiar world around us. It is the role of art to make us see the world anew by presenting it to us from an unusual angle. As the marvellously named Formalist critic Victor Shklovsky put it, 'Habitualization devours works, clothes, furniture, one's wife, and fear of war... art exists that one may recover the sensation of life...' [1]. On a smaller literary scale, metaphor is also a way of seeing something afresh through the comparison with something unexpectedly similar.

They say that travel broadens the mind. Encountering different cultures, landscapes, people, language, food and so forth furnishes us with more possibilities and options for how to live our lives. Travel can also do

[1] Quoted in Lodge, *The Art of Fiction*, p.53
[2] Strand & Boland, *The Making of a Poem*, p. 7

something analogous to defamiliarisation and to metaphor: Stepping out of our usual lives and cultures, experiencing something different, helps us to reflect on our life and culture in a comparative light. If you've holidayed somewhere hot and arid in the summer, for instance, I expect on your return you appreciated afresh the greenness and lushness of the English landscape. (You might also have noticed the rain, but then it's pretty hard to forget that.) What is homesickness if not a realisation of one's love for a place we normally take for granted?

The first three breezy stanzas of Flynn's poem express the sort of wanderlust that drives those lucky enough to have gap years abroad. That this is a common feeling is expressed immediately, 'like many folk'. The informal, relaxed register suits the context of backpacking to far-flung places. The jaunty rhythm and decisive, positive vibe carry through these stanzas. For example, the emphatic series of monosyllables in 'I thought: Yes. This is how/ to live'. Enjambment between lines and over stanza breaks adds to the poem's energetic forward momentum. Palpable excitement is in the air:

- exotic place names are mentioned, making the idea of travelling concrete - 'the Sherpa pass'; 'Krakow'; 'Zagreb'; 'Siberian' all tumble out in a breathless list
- three figures of speech are used in quick succession - the spine 'like a meridian', the airport like a 'cell', the idea clear as a 'tannoy'
- the poet is inspired into clever paradox - finding herself ('destiny') in losing herself ('anonymity').
- most of the lines are also short and zippy, as one idea leads quickly on to the next. There are only two full stops, one of which is internal to a line, so that when we arrive at the second, after 'destiny', it is the first time really that the poem has paused to catch its breath.

2.
What's the effect of the irregular within the regular form?
Though the poem is arranged in quatrains, the first three stanzas are strikingly

irregular. There are some very long and some very short lines, the shortest, rather audaciously, is just the tail-end fragment of a word, '-mity'. There is an unusual rhyme scheme too, with the first two lines forming a couplet in each of the first two stanzas, before this pattern reverses in the third. The change in the pattern creates sonically a sense of completion of this first section of the poem. It's as if the youthful exuberance to travel expressed by the words is barely contained by the poem's form, as if the stanzas and their good lieutenants the punctuation are straining to keep the zestfulness in order. What do you make of the striking use of 'mity' as a line? Does it suggest an exuberant devil-may-careness in the narrator, breaking words and rules wherever she fancies? Or might the forcing of the word into the rhyme pattern by breaking it in two signal something running counter to the poem's overt enthusiasm? The latter idea could be supported by the vague, rather wishy-washiness of the phrase 'some kind of destiny'. As we come to the end of the third stanza there are hints that despite her apparent enthusiasm, the poet is having reservations. Or perhaps between the end of stanza three and the opening of four a significant period of time has flashed by and the speaker is now older and wiser. Such a reading suggests another way of interpreting the opening stanzas with a kind of double perspective.

The retrospective nature of the narration ['when first I saddled'] indicates that the poem is written at a later stage looking back at how the narrator used to feel about travel. Hence it combines the innocent enthusiasm they felt at the

time with a later, more experienced, reflective self-awareness. It is the latter perspective we pick up as a tonal counter strain to the surface enthusiasm.

Slight subtextual unease prepares us subtly for the shift in the fourth stanza. We learn that despite all her energetic zeal the poet either hasn't set off on amazing adventures or that her days of backpacking are now over. The pace of the poem slows, lines lengthen, the sense of forward momentum dissipates. Stanzas four and five are structured around contrast. Exotic locations the poet could have travelled to, 'Larium', 'Western Union', 'Madison', 'Milwaukee' are evoked only to make the contrast with reality of being in a post office more poignant. And, instead of doing exciting, extraordinary things in exciting, extraordinary places, such as catching an American 'Greyhound' bus, the poet is doing crushingly boring, everyday, ordinary chores - paying 'bills' or a 'giro', doing her 'laundry'. Whereas at the start of the poem, the speaker had seemed master of her destiny, even if her language appeared in constant danger of running away from her, she does not seem to know now how she arrived at this particular impasse. The sense of deflation is nicely captured in a neatly turned couplet:

'...I am less likely/ to be catching a Greyhound from Madison to Milwaukee/ than to be doing some overdue laundry'

Though, as we recognised in the first three stanzas there seems to be a counter strain running against the overt meaning of the words. Here, for example, there's a bounciness to the rhythm, reinforced by a run of 'e' rhymes, from 'likely' through to 'beyond me'. Perhaps things are not so bad after all. Again, this undercurrent prepares us nicely for the turnaround that will come at the end of the poem.

Quizzically, the poet suggests some possible explanations for a seemingly disappointing turn of events - 'whether' it was x reason or y. Yet 'why' she is where she is really 'beyond' her understanding. It appears she has ended up somewhere unexciting without making any definite choice to be there, a feeling not uncommon to most of us at some points in our lives. When we are young life can seem full of endless opportunities. As we get older, generally speaking, our life choices become more constrained.

One word in the poem is given a line to itself. Perhaps it is the single, most important word in *The Furthest Distance I've Travelled*: 'However'. This is the hinge word on which the whole poem turns.

3.

A Pair of pants

Can you think of anything less romantic, exotic, thrilling or adventurous than washing a pair of someone else's old pants? I'm struggling to. In the introduction to this book we mentioned the idea of literary language and diction appropriate to the rarefied sphere of poetry. I'd wager as a noun the word 'pants' hadn't been used in any poem until at least the second half of the twentieth century. Only 'y-fronts' could beat in it in a competition for least poetic word. 'Sports sock' might run it close. Anyhow, more than enough about unpoetic pants and socks. The list of places in the opening stanzas is replaced now with  a matching list of everyday 'throwaway' ephemera, the ordinary junk we take no notice of, usually, stuff we find in back pockets or down the backs of sofas. Small stuff too, things we easily discard. Flynn uses a simple, but powerful metaphor to flip over our perceptions. In the final two stanzas the lines lengthen as the poem moves into more ruminative, reflective mode. A sense of order and balance is generated by the movement into a repeated, regular rhyme scheme and more even line length. Flynn implies that habit can make us take the people around us for granted. We should see them, she suggests, as being like the countries or continents. Poignantly the poet conveys the importance of valuing our interactions with other people, embedded in these ordinary objects. For this throwaway stuff has value, it is 'what survives/ of holidaying briefly, in other people's 'lives'.

Are you convinced? Is she right? Do you admire her stoicism? Or is the end of the poem an unconvincing rationalisation of the decisions made, or not made? At first the metaphor of holidaying in other people's lives seems apt. But what if your holidays do not feature the adventure of back-packing, but comprise lounging on a beach soaking up the sun?

Crunching

Crunching a poem is a quick and interesting way of reducing the text to its most significant words. Only one word is chosen per line of the poem. I recommend you have a go at completing this task on your own at first and then compare your crunching with your peers. Through discussion, see if you can come to an agreed class crunched version. Then compare your version to mine.

Of course, the crunching process can be usefully repeated all the way down to the most important few words, or even a single word, in a poem. And it can be easily adapted: Crunching the best lines, or images, crunching through picking out all the nouns or adjectives or verbs, and so forth.

The Furthest Distance... crunched:

RUCKSACK – BACK – SPINE – MERIDIAN – YES – BETWEEN – ZAGREB – AIRPORTS – CLEAR – RESTLESSNESS – DESTINY – WHETHER – THREATS – NOT – LITHUANIAN – BILLS – GIRO – HOLDALL – GREYHOUND – LAUNDRY – BEYOND – HOWEVER – ROUTINE – PANTS – STOWAWAY – FLOWER – KNOW – VALENTINES – TRAVELLED – PEOPLE – LIVES

A further crunch...

RUCKSACK – RESTLESSNESS – DESTINY – THREATS – LAUNDRY – PANTS – PEOPLE - LIVES

With its emphasis on the value of human relationships, *The Furthest Distance...* could be compared to many of the other poems in the anthology. *A Minor Role* springs to mind because of its similar championing of the ordinary and seemingly significant. *Material* also shares the use of something seemingly insignificant to reveal significance. The innocence/ experience theme and idea of growing up connects it to *To My Nine-Year-Old Self*, while the wry, knowing and winningly self-deprecating narrative voice might make an interesting comparison to Armitage's *Chainsaw* poem.

Roderick Ford, *Giuseppe*

1.

Roderick Ford is a Welsh poet who spent much of his youth living in locations as disparate as the UK, Australia, and Africa. Whilst he was a young adult, in the 1970s, he received what he described as 'inappropriate' treatment for Asperger's Syndrome, which wasn't diagnosed until much later; he spent much of his time under the influence of heavy tranquilisers and started writing poetry when his medication was stopped.

Giuseppe comes from his poetry collection ***The Shoreline of Falling*** (2005). Ford's work frequently explores the isolating effects of autism; the image of the solitary and voiceless figure is one that Ford revisits. In particular, the liminal existence of the mermaid - half human, and half fish - depicts that fragile membrane between social interaction and isolation that is the hallmark of an autistic existence. This is also shown elsewhere in the collection; in *Lay my Corpse* the human body is described as being consumed by nature, and its voice replaced by the wordless *'conversations of the laughing dead'*.

One of the haunting tensions throughout Ford's work is the contradiction of using words to depict voicelessness. In his poem *Miss Johnson*, the title character never speaks; 'she slept on a cushion in an old wicker basket / and used a lace hankie to cover herself'. In *Giuseppe*, the mermaid only 'screamed like a woman in terrible fear', because 'she was only a fish, and fish can't speak'. This struggle to be heard is challenged by the lucidity of his writing, showing how a poet can use words to distil and piece together an otherwise murky and confusing reality.

2.
Using biography

When you read a poem, sometimes it is easy to pinpoint parts of the writing that you think directly link to another piece of information you might know about the poet's life. <u>Do you think it is important to know about the poet's personal background to write most effectively about his or her work?</u>

In this way, *Giuseppe* presents us with an interesting dilemma. We know that Ford is diagnosed as being on the autistic spectrum; people with autism or Asperger's find it difficult to socialise and communicate in the same way that people without these conditions do. <u>Therefore, is the central character of the mermaid in this poem - and her inability to speak - meant to represent the pain of struggling to communicate in the same way that everyone else does?</u> If this is the case, we could, perhaps, look at the poem as being in the 'confessional' genre - a movement of poetry that emerged in the USA in the late 1950s. As we mentioned in the introduction to this book, confessional poetry explores personal experience directly, often delving into and exposing trauma and the inner, private self.

Maybe Ford, in this poem, is expressing what it is like to be spoken for by others - the frustration and anger of not being able to get involved with other people in quite the same way that everyone seems to. However, there are always problems with using a strictly biographical reading, and in any case there are no marks for referring to biographical context in the Edexcel marking scheme. Whilst this is important for your own understanding of the poem, the mark scheme wants you to be able to investigate the 'nuts and bolts' of the text, for which context can inform reading - but only after you have read it and taken it apart first.

Biography might be significant, but all poetry should be judged by its internal qualities of imagery, structure and language. Using these guidelines, another reading of the poem becomes clear; Ford takes his own experience of having Asperger's Syndrome and combines it with the image of the violated female body to suggest many different possible things - for example, that to take away a woman's voice, or to speak over her, is an act of violence.

3.

How can we interpret the imagery in this poem?

Anyone who has read *Captain Corelli's Mandolin* (Louis de Bernières, 1994) might well recognise the imagery of the Mediterranean setting of WWII – 'where the bougainvillea grows so well', by 'the dry and dusty ground'. Here the image of the lushness of nature springing after the sterility of war and death is one of hope, of renewal after terrible suffering. Important images that arise in the poem form an overall conceit (an extended metaphor used throughout a poem), in this case, the theme of being silenced by violence during wartime.

The first is the allusion to the Holocaust, an allusion which runs throughout. This is expressed through references to human experimentation:

- 'when they took a ripe golden roe /from her side, the doctor said /this was proof she was just a fish'
- the taking of wedding rings from the corpses of Jews – 'someone tried to take her wedding ring'
- and the rationale that those who were 'simple' (or what Himmler called 'undesirable') deserved to be removed from society, 'butchered on the dry and dusty ground'.

This leads onto another important theme,

that of violence towards women. A feminist reading of this poem would underline the narrative, as shown here, of the treatment of women as an oppressed group. Presented as a sort of monster, a 'mermaid', through the poem's male perspective, the female character is thus made unfamiliar, non-human and 'other'. And this 'othering', coupled with her lack of a voice, frees the male characters to treat the female with savage, cannibalistic violence. The female character's horrific death is a compact analogy of the kind of sexual violence and torture used against women in times of war, which functions as an enforced imprinting of one party's, or tribe's, ethnicity, onto the women of the other side. Through forced reproduction, this means that one race gains prevalence and biological power over another; exactly the goal of the Holocaust in seeking to imprint a 'right' ethnicity and to destroy those whom they saw as 'sub-human'. Through making her a fantastical creature, Ford also asks us to find the familiar in the strange and otherworldly. Have a look at the poem again and see who you think are the more powerful or monstrous people here.

Is it the humans, or the mermaid?

This is another way in which the overarching theme of silence is achieved, which again would sit with a feminist criticism of the text. The mermaid, just as sub-human as other socially oppressed groups, can only make noises within the parameters of what is already stereotypically 'female'. Hence she 'screams like a woman in terrible fear'. Her way of expressing herself is reduced to visceral, hysterical sounds, the repeated brash vowel sounds of 'e' and 'I'- 'she', 'fish', 'fish', 'screamed', 'terrible' and 'fear'- supporting this. The middle ground, or 'liminality', between being fish and human is an analogy for women in general, who historically have been seen as defined in relation to to their bodies (the word 'hysteria' comes from the Latin *hystera* for 'womb') and more grounded in 'animal' instincts than men. Though she is called a 'mermaid' and has 'golden roe' taken from her side, the weight of details imply the victim was a real woman:

- 'She was so simple'

- 'One of her hands'
- 'Her throat was cut'
- 'She screamed'
- 'Wedding ring'.

The female character is literally 'butchered', 'cooked and fed to the troops' who have been 'starved'. Her offspring are removed in the strange fashion of a caesarean section, the 'ripe golden roe' coming from her side just as the blood comes from the side of Christ, or Eve from the side of Adam. However, the image here is not redemptive or generative; it ends in death and sterility. Ford uses the many different treatments of the woman's body to explore the different ways in which we can be physically silenced.

4.

Form and structure

Throughout the poem, metre and form are used to underline a general feeling of unrest and unease. For example, the first stanza is filled with irregular lines, the beginning often 'tripping' over a few syllables to get to the first stressed one (stressed beats are underlined): 'in the courtyard behind the aquarium'. However, the two lines that are perfectly in even metre are:

'the only captive mermaid in the world / was butchered on the dry and dusty ground'

The first line, built evenly and smoothly evokes beauty, yet quickly moves onto the finality of 'butchered' and the awkwardly jilting 'doctor, a fishmonger, and certain others'.

There are three monosyllabic lines: 'While her throat was cut'; 'and the ring stayed put' and 'or which I thank God'. The last one ends the whole poem with a distressing, emphatic finality, although the 'thank God' could, of course, indicate that the uncle feels shame, therefore making it less distressing. The poem starts and ends with the characters of Uncle Giuseppe and God respectively, the latter of whom is remarkably absent in the rest of the poem. The fact that 'the priest... held one of her hands / while her throat was cut' suggests an image of a hospital chaplain, but also, arguably, of the priest as witness to a martyrdom; either way, Ford goes to no efforts to make him seem 'godly' or pious. The sudden turn towards God at the end of the poem adds a new dimension. If the poet hadn't written the last line, the reader would be forced to judge the actions of the characters in relation to each other, and to their setting. By inserting God into the structure at the very end, the narrator implies that there is a different system of morality by which these characters should be judged.

5.

Chinese whispers?

Another important aspect to note is the narrative voice. Ford does not use his narrator as a 'fly-on-the-wall' figure, in the middle of the action and developing along with the events of the poem. Instead, the whole scenario is talked about as being far in the past. Like an archaeological dig, little bits of information are uncovered for the reader to piece together a version of events. In fact, the reader is actually hearing this improbable story third-hand as it comes from the uncle, to the nephew (narrator), to the reader. The effect of these 'chinese whispers' is not only to remove the story further from us, but also to emphasise the fantastical nature of the characters - the very issue of whether or not we can ever receive an unbiased version of historical events becomes important. It is clear that the mermaid's vulnerability is something that brings sorrow and discomfort to both the narrator and the other characters. However, it is not written in the strict form of an elegy, which the Greeks structured as having an opening lament, followed by praise and admiration, then a consoling finish. Do you think the poem has any consoling effect for the reader- is it supposed to have an unsettled ending? Does the form allow for there to be anything other than incomplete snapshots of people, times and places?

The fact that the bougainvillea grows so well suggests growth and redemption from death and sterility, relating to the re-birth of individuals, communities and countries after the World Wars. However, the involvement of both medical and religious authorities, specifically not the armed forces on the front line, implies that every person, and all parts of society, could be seen as implicit in wartime violence.

Giuseppe crunched:

UNCLE – SICILY – COURTYARD – MERMAID – BUTCHERED – PRIEST – THROAT – CUT – SCREAMED – FISH – ROE – BURIAL – WEDDING RING – COOKED – FED – GOD

The poem explores the images of violence and consumption, and as such could be compared to many of poems in the anthology. *Eat Me* also makes the connection between the female body and food, in a more visceral and graphic way. *Effects* looks at the physical legacy of dying, a useful poem if you want to explore in a deeper way the relationship between the dead and those who are left behind. Finally, *The Lammas Hireling* also features a fantastical creature and also explores human mistrust and violence towards an unfamiliar 'other'.

Seamus Heaney, *Out of the Bag*

1.

Fatefully dubbed the greatest Irish poet since W. B. Yeats, Seamus Heaney (1939-2013) was a Nobel Prize winning writer who was probably the most famous poet of his generation. Dealing with growing up in a rural home, Heaney's early poems were characterised by the intense, onomatopoeic physicality of their language. The disturbing and challenging poems in his 1975 collection **North** shifted attention away from the formation of self to the turbulent political times in which Heaney lived and, in particular, The Troubles. After winning the Nobel Prize for literature in 1995, Heaney's poetic focus and mode shifted again, this time into something more lyrical and celebratory, into what the poet himself called a poetry concerned with 'crediting marvels'. No doubt the Good Friday Agreement and the progress made by the Northern Ireland peace process contributed to the sense of release and the lifting of a weight from Heaney's poetry.

Out of the Bag comes from Heaney's elegiac 2001 collection **Electric Light**. Described on its dust jacket as a book about 'origins...the places where things start from, the ground of understanding', *Electric Light* depicts Heaney's wide-ranging travels over the maps of his memory. Places such as his family home in Ireland, ancient Greece and the violent fenland world of *Beowulf*, which Heaney had recently translated are peopled with literary tutelary spirits, such as Virgil and Dante, as well as the ghosts of recently deceased fellow writers and friends, such as Ted Hughes and Joseph Brodsky.

In **The Loose Box** from this collection Heaney quotes an earlier Irish poet, Patrick Kavanagh, a major influence on him, on the importance of place and of the effect of writing about it; 'the main thing is/ an inner restitution, a purchase come by/ pacing it in words that you feel/ you've found your feet in what 'surefooted' means/ and in the ground of your understanding'. In another poem, **Perch**, Heaney writes about how the fish within a river is 'on hold/ in the everything flows and steady go of the world'. Like other poems in *Electric Light, Out of the Bag,* is characterised by tensions between fluidity and solidity, fragmentation and interconnection, fear as well as joy. In the poem Heaney seeks to hold on to and hold together disparate pieces of the past, not least in order to make sense of the present.

2.

Cohesion and coherence

The term cohesion refers to the way texts are stuck together by shared features. A text is cohesive when its constituent elements link through some form of repetition. Coherence refers to cohesion that makes sense, where ideas link to other ideas in a logical and followable sequence. Hence a text can be cohesive, but not coherent, but it cannot be coherent without being cohesive. At first, it seems thay *Out of the Bag* is only cohesive; a collection of disparate memories is forced together through a shared tercet form and a mesh of language. Notice, for example, the repetition of similar words, sometimes unusually close together, such as 'disappear' and 'reappear' in the first stanza, 'insides' and 'inside' in the second, 'came' and 'come' in the fifth. At other times, similar words build linguistic bridges spanning time and place, linking the poem's various narratives. Hence 'came' and 'disappear' at the start of the poem are echoed in the fourth section; 'precincts' in the third also crops up in the fourth and the key word 'incubation' appears both in the second and last sections. Cohesion creates a holding on, a holding together. Only through a closer reading does it become evident that despite its tendency towards fragmentation the poem is also, in fact, coherent.

3.

The sublime

What are your own sources of creativity and imaginative inspiration?
From where, from what and from whom do your best ideas come?

These questions lie at the heart of *Out of Bag's* meditation on origins and the mystery of creativity.

Heaney acknowledged his literary debt to the Romantic poets and, in particular, to William Wordsworth, using the following lines from Wordsworth's *The Prelude* in his collection *North*:

'Fair seedtime had my soul, and I grew up
Fostered alike by beauty and by fear.'

The painting on the left, by Caspar David Friedrich, is called *Wanderer Above the Sea Fog* and expressed the Romantic conceptualisation of the sublime. For the Romantics, inspiration springs from an individual artist's encounters with lofty, awesome, natural experiences. For the Romantics the sublime had a double aspect, containing beauty, but also terror, both, or either, of which could fire the creative imagination. We can see traces of their thinking about the positive dimension of terror in our modern usage of *terrific* as a positive term. In contrast, horror, which the Romantics believed shrinks rather than expands the soul, has no such positive cognate.

Heaney's poem finds inspiration in memories of childhood, the love of his mother, in the classical past, in the wisdom of other writers, in remembered beauty. But also in the child's terror of the Doctor and in the adult Heaney's fear of aging and illness.

4.
The doctor
As Heaney's poem is arranged in four interconnected parts, it seems simplest

to deal with each part in turn before considering the overall effect of them together. Part one is a meditation on the mystery of origins narrated from a small child's perspective. Heaney's characteristic close concentration on a specific object to reveal the whole is evident in his focus on the doctor's bag. Alongside the very specific visual imagery, comparing the bag's interior colour to that of a dog's, Heaney utilises other aspects of language to bring the memory to vivid life:

'Its lined *insides*
(The colour of a spaniel's *inside* lug)'

Alliteration of 'l' and liquidy 's' sounds run through the line, supported by assonance of the light 'i' sound. The solidly monosyllabic, Anglo-Saxon sounding noun, 'lug', is specific both in terms of part of the dog and, as a dialect word, in terms of place. Heaney fans may also recognise the word from his most famous early poem **Digging**, so that the word forges an intertextual chain back to beginning of the poet's oeuvre.

As we commented on earlier, words are repeated with slight variations in a marked and insistent fashion. As well as 'inside', other words are repeated at least twice - 'spaniel', 'colour', 'bag', 'wind', 'lined'. Consecutive words rhyme in 'nosy' and rosy' and phrases echo sonically each other, such as 'saved for him' and 'savoured by him'. Tactile imagery - 'soft hands', 'satin', 'lukewarm' and the lovely 'sud-luscious' - combines with visual - 'gleam' and 'highlights' - and the olfactory - 'a whiff of disinfectant' to generate an intimate sense of physical reality.

Until three quarters of the way through part one, the doctor is presented in a similar way to the other various masters of their craft who appear regularly in Heaney's work. To the child, the doctor is a powerful, commanding and compelling presence, 'like a hypnotist' casting a spell of concentration. Or a magician who performs miraculous tricks, making objects appear and disappear, the coup de theatre of which, of course, is the conjuring of a baby. The only hint of the terror to come is the ominous reference to his exit as 'darken(ing) the door'.

When the doctor catches the child's eye in his own glacial gaze, Heaney's

imagination takes flight. In a startling metaphor the eyes are transformed into 'peep holes' to a 'locked room'. Traditionally eyes are considered the windows to the soul, implying that this locked room is the doctor's soul. The poem's perspective stares through the child's terrified eyes at this place of forbidden knowledge. We witness a scene from a horror film; some sort of perverse dissecting or torture chamber where human body parts hang, neatly, on 'steel hooks', like pieces of meat, and blood 'dreeps in the sawdust'. Fantasy and reality fuse in the unsettling image of the rosebud the Doctor wears, as if a secret badge of monstrosity, resembling a child's 'cock'.

5.

Academia

At first part two seems entirely unrelated. Like a massive cross-cut in a film, the scene jumps across space and time, from Heaney's childhood home in Ireland and his wide-eyed, boyish perspective, to the theatre at Epidaurus in Greece (shown in the photograph below) many years later. Linguistically the poem now shifts dramatically too, into the learned discourse of a literary academic.

This academic discourse is signalled from the outset by the switch into Latin, by the references to influential intellectuals (who the reader is assumed to know), by the reference to the Ancient Greek, Asclepius, and the school-teacherly parenthetical explanatory note: '(called *asclepions*)'. Google Peter Levi and you'll discover he was an Oxford professor of poetry. Graves refers to the influential poet and expert on Greek myths, Robert Graves, and Asclepius was an ancient Greek god of medicine. Asclepius's daughter, Hygia, was a goddess of health. Clearly we have moved from the home to the academy.

The nature of the discussion of how a theatre is like a hospital, art like medicine and theatre like religious ritual is also more self-consciously elevated, philosophical and reflective. The repetition of the word 'doctor' in 'doctus' links parts one and two cohesively and we come to understand that both sections are concerned with the creation of life. The birth of a human child in part one is replaced by the birth of creative art. The process of creation here is made more explicit:

ritual ➔ altered state of consciousness (here sleep) ➔ epiphany or revelation ➔ meeting the god (moment of creation)

Seamus Heaney rarely used ellipsis in his poetry, so the fact that he employs this device twice in the same poem is significant. The meeting with 'the god...' is followed by another memory, this time only a brief snatch of being part of a procession. It is unclear if this memory is the result of the meeting of not. Memory gives way to memory in quickening succession as narrative is enfolded within narrative. The cohesive link is the change of consciousness signalled by 'nearly fainted'. The poem becomes disorientating, giddily close to fragmenting, almost incoherent. It is not clear, for example, where Heaney is when he bends to pull some grass. And within this memory is folded another altered state of consciousness in the form of a hallucination that loops the narrative back to Doctor Kerlin and Heaney's childhood.

Through this vision, the doctor is presented here as an awesome Zeus-like creator figure, fashioning human beings with his 'large', 'big' hands and miraculously bringing them 'swimming' to life. After the intensity of this revelation and creation, like after the meeting with a god, the poet is left 'blinded with sweat/ blinking and shaky'. In classical literature the wind is associated with animation and the forces of creativity. It is therefore entirely fitting that post-creative crisis the light is 'windless'.

Part three is linked through the reference to 'bits of grass' and to illnesses that are perhaps beyond the restitutive and curative powers of poetry. Again place and time are uncertain and slippery. Presumably, for instance, the posting off of the grass occurred at a later time. As if shaken by his experiences, the poet wants 'nothing more' than to rest, 'to lie down' and to be visited by the goddess of health. Significantly, Hygia is associated by Heaney with illumination and vision - she is the 'very eye of the day', she brings clarity and she is a 'haven of light'. Notice how her special status is indicated by the poem's language lifting off into metaphor.

Whereas the impact of revelation of the male deity was disturbing and frightening, the female deity is imagined as benign and soothing. Whereas the poet was 'blinded' after the first revelation, the goddess and his mother bring 'vision'. The stark contrast is underscored by the reference to doors. Heaney's second collection of poems was titled *Door into the Dark* and in it Heaney used the door as a symbol for a gateway into the unknown. Where Dr Kerlin darkened the door, implying a blocking of perception and access, Hygia is an 'undarkening door', a curative gateway of, and to, light. Perhaps the female deity is the beautiful aspect of the sublime, the flip side of the terrible aspect represented by the Doctor.

6.

Home again

We circle back to Heaney's childhood and his home in section four. In memory time can curve, move forwards and backwards, fold in on itself. Linguistically this looping is signalled by the verb 'came' whose simplicity hides the mysteries of creation. The language here drops down to the ordinary and conversational, suitable for an intimate interior, domestic scene with mother and child. Once again repetitive patterns of diction are evident: 'I stand alone' – 'standing'; 'again and again'; 'peering, appearing'. Words from earlier in the poem reappear, most significantly 'doctor', 'precinct', 'asleep' and 'incubating'.

In a later poem from *Electric Light* Heaney celebrates a bridge for its 'holding action'. It is, Heaney, suggests 'strain' and 'tension' that actually holds the bridge 'steady' and makes it 'strong'. In *Out of the Bag* the poet performs this holding action, connecting memories, stories and ideas together, taking the strain of keeping whole this large narrative arc in place, making the poem strong, he hopes, through the balancing of its internal tensions.

Time shifts again. Recalling the opening lines of T.S. Eliot's **Four Quartets** ('Time present and time past/ Are both perhaps present in time future /And time future contained in time past') the poem switches into the present tense, an eternal now of memory. Heaney had written a series of loving, tender poems to his mother in a series called Glanmore sonnets, so the end of the poem is a return in another intertextual sense too.

Revealed is a tender, quiet, domestic scene. The poet '(with) standing the passage of time' so that this memory seems 'pure reality' - things are happening 'for real' and he is alone with his mother who is 'asleep'. As he had done as a thurifer (a senior altar server carrying the incense) the small boy acts as willing helper, here in this more intimate, personal creative process, allowed access into a a 'precinct of vision' through his mother's smile. But her final gentle words to him continue to obscure the process of creation and underplay her own central role in it. Significantly it is the male doctor she credits for the creation of the baby.

7.

Why the characteristic doubling of language in the poem? To me the answer lies in the concept of the sublime and, in particular, its double aspect of beauty and terror. The poem is a rumination on origins and creativity that sets an apparently potent and disturbing male form against a gentler, but actually more powerful and generative female one.

What of the form of the poem? Why tercets?
Generally Heaney's early poems are characterised by his use of large blocks, almost slabs of stanzas. Tercets are less monumental, more delicate, sparer and leaner forms. Dante's *The Divine Comedy* was a key influence on Heaney and he seems to have picked up the tercet form from the great Italian writer. However, Dante's tercets are linked one to another in a continuous chain, forged through a strict rhyme scheme called terza rima. Eschewing rhyme and unmetred, Heaney's tercets are much looser constructions. Thus a tension runs through the poem, a strain between loosening irregularity and solidifying regularity: The consistent use of tercets helps unify the disparate parts of a poem that at times veers close to breaking into fragments.

As this is a long, complex poem, I'm not going to take a word from every line. Here's the poem crunched, section by section:

CAME – DISAPPEAR – REAPPEAR – HANDS – INSIDES – LUG – EMPTY – HYPNOTIST – WIND – DARKEN – KEEL – CAME – ALSO – AGAIN – GLEAM – SATIN – WATER – SUD-LUSCIOUS – SAVOURED – TOWELLED – HELD – SQUIRED – EYES – HYPERBOREAN – LOCKED – SWABBED – HOOKS – BLOOD – PARTS – STRUNG – COCK – BUTTONHOLE

POETA – SANCTUARIES – SHRINES – CURE – POETRY – I –

SANATORIUM – INCUBATION – RITUAL – GOD – GROGGY – PROCESSION – FAINTED – HALLUCINATED – DOCTOR – INDEX – LAVED – MIRACULUM – BITS – HANDS – BLINDED – WINDLESS – CHEMOTHERAPY – COME – LEAVE – PRECINCTS – TEMPLE – NOTHING – SEEDED – EYE – HYGEIA – HAVEN – ROOM – REALITY – TIME – DOCTOR – AGAIN – INCUBATING – PEERING – EYES – VISION – ENTER – TRIUMPH – THINK – BABY – ASLEEP.

Other poems exploring mother to child relationships include *Genetics, Effects* and *On her Blindness*. The meditative, philosophical nature of *Out of the Bag* could be compared with *History* and its concern with the significance of the past.

Alan Jenkins, *Effects*

According to one of Alan Jenkins' poetic 'elders and betters' his 'subject was loss' and he should 'stay with that'. He certainly stays with it in *Effects*, a poem of devastating everyday observation and desolate loss. Now, while the 'I' voice in the poem could most obviously be identified with Jenkins himself it need not be seen as so personal. Either way, the personal voice intensifies the universality of the experience. The effects of the title are not released, mimetically, until the very last line of this 50-line meditation, but the poetic effects are felt from the unsettling first line with its 'scarred' 'hand'. Emily Dickinson insisted that 'art is a house that tries to be haunted' and here Jenkins achieves the type of lingering literature that Dickinson would admire.

1.
Ephemeral effects
This haunting quality produced by the poem derives from its everyday trivialities, which become torqued into something greater through Jenkins' transformative verse. Not only is the subject matter difficult to confront but the manner of Jenkins' poetic exploration is also deeply unsettling. I suppose this is very much the point. Nowhere is this more acute than in his unavoidable message about the distinctly ephemeral nature of our existence.

The poem condenses the aging process his mother endures through the detailed descriptions of her hands. The poem begins with her 'scarred' hand,

testifying to her durability, her enduring strength, the triumph of the physical over reality. Rather than weakness, such scars celebrate the robustness of a body capable of withstanding years of 'shopping,' 'slicing' and 'scrubbing'. Whilst undeniably domestic, the poem suggests a quiet heroism in the everyday as these trivial tribulations originate from 'love', albeit an 'old-fashioned' love, but love nevertheless.

The alliteration of 'I held her hand' with its softness resurfaces much later in the poem in line 44 in a subtle, yet vitally, different way. It becomes 'the hand I held,' which immediately implies a compelling change through the loss of the previous possessive pronoun 'her.' Such a minute difference dehumanises the mother figure, the hand becoming a mere object. By this stage in the poem, the strong 'scarred' hands of the beginning have 'become blotched and crinkled,' two adjectives that foreground their poor condition and delicacy. The connotations of 'crinkled', in particular, imply a paper-like quality that captures her intense vulnerability just before death.

2.

Sentimental synecdoche

A fancy Greek term for how the part can be substituted for the whole (i.e. 'sails' for 'ships' and 'suits' for 'business types') the poem excels in its equation of mundane everyday objects with the recently deceased. Jenkins vividly captures how ordinary personal effects can contain such latent power through their ability to store vast reservoirs of memory.

The speaker will not have access to the hands of his beloved mother in the future. But he/she will have the things that adorned them: 'her rings' and her 'classic ladies' model, gold strap' 'watch'. Both items replace the mother after death's annihilating effect. In fact, the mini-mystery of the watch that 'was gone' propels the poem into a series of episodic accounts that convey her descent into senility. Jenkins uses anaphora (the repetition of 'not' at the start of poetic lines) as a stimulus to memorialisation. Seeing the dead mother's hand without the 'gold strap' watch compels the speaker to think of that same hand with the watch.

The sequence of memories triggered by the watchless hand is a heart-breaking condensation of the mother's abject loneliness: From the death of her husband, to her 'scotch' soaked failure to cope, to her admittance to 'the psychiatric ward'. The poem ends by bestowing huge value on 'the little bag of her effects'. Their value does not come from their status as independent objects in their own right; rather it is their dependence on their previous owner that renders them valuable. Essentially worthless personal effects become repositories of the past, makers of memory that bring the dead back to life, if only in the most figurative of ways.

3.
The taste of disdain

The oddly sour relationship between the mother and child is conspicuous in *Effects*. The poet is unflinching in his refusal to idealise the deceased; there are no funereal clichés such as 'she was the best mum a son could ever have'. Admirably, the minutiae of life are depicted as sharply and realistically as those of aging and death. The reality of their relationship is characterised by the son's 'disdain' and 'contempt' for his mother.

The speaker's mother is 'old-fashioned' and backwards in her insistence on 'bland' 'English' cuisine. She has not, and presumably cannot, move with the times. This is a woman who embodies the narrow spirit of the Little Englander, in how she prefers the 'familiar flavours' of the 'bland' to 'funny foreign stuff'. Jenkins' wealth of f-sounds introduces an element of the conflict between the two. Her designation of anywhere outside England as 'abroad', which Jenkins is careful to put into speech marks, suggests a closed-minded woman stuck in the past. Her voice is captured in tiny, trivial soundbites that capture her ordinariness.

Not that the speaker comes across as noble character either. The poem is surprisingly candid in this regard. Here we have a man full of snobbish 'disdain' and 'contempt' for a woman no more to blame for being a product of her time than he is. Telling little details like when he confesses to 'all the weeks I didn't come' in the traumatic loss of her husband betray a cold, uncaring personality. Even when he recognises her domestic toil as 'giving love the only way she knew' he cannot help his 'disdain' for her backward ways and unsophisticated interests. Most damning is the heartrending moment at the end of the poem where she begs him to *'Please don't leave'*. Jenkins' only italicisation of her speech and also his use of a forceful molossus [three stressed beats in a row] maximises the vulnerability of her distress. Tellingly, this is deflated by the casual admission: 'But of course I left'. There is something too barbed about the mother's remark about how he 'grew up and learned contempt' that implies intense disappointment with the adult speaker. Not only do we get access to his disdain, but also her disdain at his disdain. It is clear that both characters in this intense drama cannot see each other without personal resentment: Jenkins places emphasis on the inability to not see through subtle repetition and variation of language i.e. 'stared unseeing', 'gulped and unseeing', 'blinked unseeing' and 'blinked and stared'. Symbolically at the end of the poem the mother 'could not [...] turn her face to see' her returning son, which implies that reconciliation never happened.

However, despite their acrimonious relationship and the lack of reconciliation, there is clearly an intense sense of bereavement. Death seems to defuse the personal antagonisms that life simply could not. Some sort of regret at this situation is suggested in how the speaker reconstructs the pathos of her demise. It is almost as if empathy is only possible after she has passed on. The painful details of her existence on the 'psychiatric ward' are nightmarish in their portrayal of an undignified, dehumanising purgatory: TVs 'blare' to mask deranged 'moans and curses'; the patients 'shuffled round, and drooled, and swore...'. Caesuras, created by the commas, imply an awkward pausing as if the speaker finds it difficult to recount such horrors. More worryingly, the ellipsis at the end of this line allows this recounting to trail off into a guilty silence as if hiding even more horrifying details.

4.

Echoes of memory

Jenkins' poem uses form to reinforce the reality of memorialising the dead. There is no place here for stately, elegiac formal patterns that bring the consolation of predictable consistency. Instead, his form espouses a regular unpredictability. While the 50 lines are written invariably in an iambic metre, this shifts from tetrameter to hexameter. The most striking formal aspect is the complex, sinuous rhyme scheme Jenkins employs. It is hard to describe completely, but the poem can be broken down into three long sections where some sort of rhyme scheme is discernible and a short final section where mono-rhyme is used conspicuously.

The rhyme scheme in these longer sections is curiously unpredictable. It is simultaneously tight and loose: Just when the ear is starting to accommodate itself to a definite pattern the poem shifts suddenly into new sounds before lurching back to previous ones. For example, take the first 9 lines. The end rhymes are: **SCARRED – WAIT – RAW – PLATE – KNEW – STEW – ATE – RINGS**, which gives a rhyme scheme of **ABCBDDBE**. There are outbursts of cross rhyme i.e. **SWORE – BAND – WORE – HAND – MORE**. Again, the ear expects a word that rhymes with 'hand' and 'band' but gets 'sleeve' instead. Additionally, Jenkins uses half-rhymes like **SCARRED** and **ABROAD** and **IF** and **WIFE** to further emphasis a woozy soundscape that seems to drift in and out of sonic focus. All in all, it gives the poem an echoing sonic unpredictability that seems to mimic the senile memory or maybe just the uncertainty of memory itself. Like a sonic déjà vu, the sound patterns feel familiar but different. Yet there are sudden bursts of clarity.

The use of sporadic mono-rhyming couplets and finally a triplet allow brief respites of certainty from the shifting sonic uncertainty that characterises the poem as a whole. In this way they mimic the memories stimulated by 'the little bag of effects' and by all objects with sentimental value. They also mimic the sudden moments of clarity experienced by the senile. Such instances are important as they can be seen to condense down the entire poem to its basic elements: **KNEW** and **STEW**; **GONE** and **ON**; **SAT** and **AT**; **SCOTCH** and **TOUCH**; **SLEEVE** and **LEAVE**; **SHE**, **SEE** and **ME**. Perhaps, fittingly, the most certainty comes at the end of the poem, where the aforementioned cross-rhyming sequence segues into a mono-rhyming couplet and triplet. Jenkins' end rhymes here suggest that the only certainty we have is death and loss.

Crunches
SCARRED – KNIVES – RAW – REDDENED – SAUCEPAN – LOVE – MEAT

– OLD-FASHIONED – RINGS – DRAWER – FADED – SCENT-SPRAYS –
'ABROAD' – NEVER – WIFE – WATCH – GONE – NEVER – YEARS –
SOAPS – COOK – ENGLISH – FAMILIAR – FOREIGN – YOUNG – SAT –
UNSEEING – INNER – HEAVED – SCOTCH – TOUCH – AGAIN – WARD –
BLINKED – DREAMT – GIRL – CONTEMPT – BLARED – MOANS – PILLS
– DROOLED – LAY – SMUDGED – CRINKLED – CLASP – FUMBLE –
PLEASE – BACK – FACE – EFFECTS

A further crunch:

SCARRED – LOVE – OLD-FASHIONED – RINGS – FADED – WIFE –
GONE – YEARS – FAMILIAR – SCOTCH – WARD – DREAMT – BLARED –
MOANS – PILLS – DROOLED – FUMBLE – PLEASE – FACE – EFFECTS

An obvious connecting poem for **_Effects_** is Adam Thorpe's **_On Her Blindness_**, which also explores the specific loss of an aging mother. Other poems featuring relationships with mothers include, **_Material_**, **_Genetics_** and **_Out of the Bag_** while **_Inheritance_** shifts the perspective to a parent's point of view. A different type of loss haunts Sean O'Brien's elegiac **_Fantasia on a Theme of James Wright_**.

Sinéad Morrissey, *Genetics*

Describe the poetic form of a villanelle in words and it sounds fiendishly difficult to write. Here are the authors of **The Making of a Poem, a Norton Anthology of Poetic Forms** giving it their best shot:

'Five stanzas occur of three lines each. They are followed by a stanza, a quatrain, of four lines. This is common to all villanelles. The first line of the first stanza serves as the last line of the second and fourth stanzas. The third line of the first stanza serves as the last line of the third and fifth stanzas. And these two refrain lines reappear to constitute the last two lines of the closing quatrain...The rhyme scheme is aba, for the first three lines of the poem. And these rhymes reappear to match and catch the refrains, throughout the villanelle. The first line of the first stanza rhymes with the third line of the fourth stanza. And so on.' [2]

 Got it? Good. So your task now is to write your own villanelle. Except that even the complex form of the villanelle seems to have bewitched even the august authors of the Norton guide. Because that's not quite right. The rhyme scheme in a villanelle is, indeed, aba, but this scheme runs through all the five three line, tercet, stanzas before finally being recycled in the concluding two lines. In other words, all the rhymes in a villanelle are composed from just two rhyme sounds. Lines, 1, 3, 4, 6, 7, 9, 10, 12, 13, 15, 16, 18 & 19 all rhyme with each other. The middle lines of each tercet, lines 2, 5, 8, 11, 14 and 17, also all rhyme with each other. Clearer now? Good. So your task in to write your own villanelle. Except that, we think it's much easier to appreciate the form of a villanelle through a visual representation, thus:

---

[2] Strand & Boland, *The Making of a Poem*, p. 7

Line 1	A	1st refrain
Line 2	B	
Line 3	A	2nd refrain
Line 4	A	
Line 5	B	
Line 6	A	1st refrain (same as line 1)
Line 7	A	
Line 8	B	
Line 9	A	2nd refrain (same as line 3)
Line 10	A	
Line 11	B	
Line 12	A	1st refrain (same as lines 1 & 6)
Line 13	A	
Line 14	B	
Line 15	A	2nd refrain (same as lines 3 & 9)
Line 16	A	
Line 17	B	
Line 18	A	1st refrain (same as lines 1,6 & 12)
Line 19	A	2nd refrain (same as lines 3, 9 & 15)

Righto. Now you've seen the form, time for you...except that, it helps to try to think of a suitable subject that might fit this elegant, looping dance of a form with its repeated patterns of lines. What we need is a subject in which there is a lot of repetition, but with variations. How about a school day? And though the form looks devilishly difficult, actually once you've got your first three lines you've already written nearly half your poem, including the last two lines. I find it helpful to write these lines in once you've got your first three in place.

And this is how I'd teach Morrissey's poem. Give the students the title and the first stanza only:

'My father's in my fingers, but my mother's in my palms.
I lift them up and look at them with pleasure –
I know my parents made me by my hands.'

So, now we can also slot lines 6, 9,1 2, 15, 18 & 19 into their fixed place in the scheme. We have our two rhyme sounds, 'a' and 'er'. Noticeably Morrissey has already bent the sound a little, or subverted the form a touch, with the assonantal rhyme 'hands' not quite harmonising with the first long 'a' sound. Why might she have done this? Certainly the slight dissonance suits the topic; the poet is trying to bring together parents who have grown apart. There's a suggestion of slight tension in the poem's sound world. Brought together in their daughter, the parents are also modified in her. So, the poem's rhymes encode the sense of continuity, but also change.

Before going on to fill in the blank lines of the poem, it's worth stopping and discussing the first tercet in more detail. Though the language looks straightforward enough, a gently surreal quality is generated by semantic ambiguity. For example, initially the apostrophes seem to indicate possession and so two nouns appear to be missing. My father's something - 'pen' perhaps? The mildly disorientating effect is sustained in the second line with ambiguous referencing of the twice used pronoun 'them'. Do the two 'thems' refer to the same thing/ person? Several different possible meaning are kept in play. <u>Which of the following do you think is most convincing?</u>

- I lift the things belonging to my father and mother and look at these
- I lift my hands and look at my hands
- I lift my parents and look at my parents
- I lift my hands and look at my parents

It's only in the last line that the ambiguity is

resolved. We realise that the apostrophes are not working to indicate possession but instead to abbreviate the nouns, so that the sense is 'my father is in my fingers'. But there's still a curious, surreal feel here; how can your father be 'in' your fingers or your mother 'in' your palms?

Now you might well be thinking I'm making quite a meal of this. And you could well be right. But I do think it's striking that although Morrissey uses very straightforward diction she manages to make language elusive, hard to pin down in terms of meanings. The double use of 'them' implies that there is no difference between her hands and her parents, they are both simply 'them'. And the overt sentiment of the poem is that her parents can be reunited in her hands. This semantic slipperiness, like the half-rhyme, conveys a counter current or undercurrent in the poem that suggests reconciliation may not be so easy, or perhaps signals the poet's awareness that the reconciliation she achieves is not completely convincing.

It's worth noting too how Morrissey flexes the villanelle form a little. With only two rhyme sounds to play with, rhymes can rather stick out awkwardly from a villanelle, making the language sound unnatural, clunky and too contrived. In an unsubtly written villanelle we will hit and notice the rhymes too much. Morrissey uses enjambment to bed down and tuck in her rhymes, so that the sentence runs over the end of the line and into the next one. In fact, the first enjambment runs stanza four into stanza five. Half-rhymes also help to dampen down the sonic echoing in the poem. The trick is to bend the form so that, despite its rigidity, it can carry the cadences of a spoken voice. Morrissey pulls off this trick with great technical aplomb.

So, now it's the students turn to flesh out the skeleton of Morrissey's poem and then to write their own villanelle on the suggested subject of a school day. By way of encouragement the author has had a go himself and you can find my villanelle at the back of this book. No peeking though, not until you've had a go yourself.

Morrissey's poem sets itself out in a series of declarative statements,

117

seemingly coolly explicating how the narrator has inherited her parents' genes and how these are evident in her body. Hence in some ways, the poem's logic tells us, the parents continue to be married in their daughter. The dominant punctuation mark is the full stop which outnumbers commas. End-stopped lines, emphasised with full stops, give each statement a definite, factual air:

'My body is their marriage register.
I re-enact their wedding with my hands'

This re-enactment even turns back time. When the narrator turns her hands into a church, her mother and father appear as if by magic, 'demure before a priest reciting psalms'. As the poem progresses the repeated refrains of the form work together like rhetorical devices - piling up they insist that reconciliation has taken place.

<u>Why did Morrissey choose the conceit of the hands as a church?</u> I think she made this choice because the 'here is a church, here is a steeple' rhyme is associated with small children. Isn't there something small childish in the poem's wish-fulfilment of reuniting parents who have grown apart? In the poem itself her parents are, indeed, reconciled. But they probably were not in real life. Hence the elegant poem is made poignant through contrast with reality. <u>Why did the poet choose the form of the villanelle to tackle this subject?</u> The form of a villanelle is like a formal dance - lines are rotated,

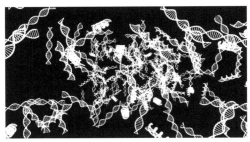 separate and then join back up again. Lines one and three for instance start close, circle each other and finish even closer together as the poem's last two lines. Hence the form embodies the idea of separating and coming back together again; separation and connection between the narrator's parents and between them and her. Perhaps there's even some analogy between the poem's shape and the twists of a genetic code. The narrator is also stuck in the desire to reconcile her parents, a

repeating emotional pattern; a need she cannot escape or move beyond. At least not until the final stanza where there's a major shift in the poem.

There is a delayed introduction of an addressee 'you' into *Genetics*. Reading the last stanza, we realise the whole poem has, in fact, been addressed to this silent presence and that the villanelle form is being employed rhetorically, to persuade this person about something important. This much is apparent from the fact that the final stanza begins with a conjunction 'so', a simple synonym for 'therefore'. This is the language of logical argument: A proposition has been advanced, demonstrated and proven and so this final stanza proffers the logical conclusion. The persuasiveness continues with the shift into imperatives. And we realise that *Genetics* is in fact a tender love poem, to the poet's parents, but also to their lover. An offer is made to be with someone and perhaps have a child with them. The tone and manner of the poem might appear cool and sophisticated; a clever conceit is manufactured from a childish rhyme and is elegantly achieved. But underneath this cleverness there's a vulnerability, a sense of loss, a poignant tenderness. And that too is persuasive.

Genetics crunched:

MY – THEM – PARENTS – REPELLED – SEPARATE – TOUCH –NOTHING – IMAGE – LEAST – SHAPE – I – MY – PARENT – MANAGE – SO – FUTURE – BEQUEATH - MAKE

Obviously in terms of theme **_Genetics_** could be compared with **Inheritance** and **Material.** Other poems about relationships with parents include **On her Blindness** and **Effects.** In terms of innovative use of a closed poetic form, **Ode to a Grayson Perry Urn** would make an interesting comparison.

Andrew Motion, *From the Journal of a Disappointed Man*

1.

This is a poem about being suspended, about being stuck in an uncertain, in-between, or liminal, state. Take the title. This informs us that the text is an extract taken from a longer piece of non-fiction. That seems straightforward enough. However, a 'journal' usually comprises factual reportage written in prose, but, this text is a poem. Moreover, check Motion's oeuvre and you'll discover that there is no extended poetic 'journal' from which this piece has been extracted. The journal of the title is, in fact, fictional. Such tricksy unreliability should put us on guard as readers – from the outset we cannot necessarily trust what we are being told in this poem, however transparent the language might appear. Uncertainty about the nature of the text raises questions too about its narrator: If we cannot rely even on the title how can we trust the testimony that follows? Is the titular character Motion himself, or a fictional alter ego? Many questions are raised in this poem, but answers are withheld. Hence the reader, like the wooden pile being lifted, and the narrator himself, is left up in the air.

The poem's 'action' confirms the theme of suspension and stasis. Though much thought and rumination goes on in the poem - about how to move the pile into the right place - it actually remains in the same place as it started in the opening lines. The 'action' of the poem is actually 'inaction'.

2.

'Clear as water'

Prosaic language invites us to lower our reading guard. This appears to be language as a window – to be looked through, not at. Immediately a chatty colloquial style is established: 'I discovered these men...'. The speaker clumsily repeats words and phrases; the second sentence includes, 'and, as I said' and a 'wooden pile, a massive affair'. Such close unnecessary repetition is a feature often found in spoken language. It would have been simple for the poet to straighten out the syntax to avoid awkward repetition. For example:

'I discovered these men driving a massive new wooden pile into the pier'

The syntactical clumsiness is, then, deliberate. The apparent artlessness of the style is designed to win our trust, invite our belief, perhaps. Other aspects of the language enhance this impression. This is plain, limpid language, stripped of any ornamentation. There is, for instance, a distinct absence of figurative imagery. And, though the poem is arranged in neat looking quatrains, it reads like prose. We have no problems decoding the sense. There's no rhyme scheme either nor any rhythmical pulse. Few sonic effects distract (or hold) our attention. No poetic enchantment is going on here, it seems. Motion appears to be doing no more than using ordinary, unremarkable language to inform us about an ordinary, unremarkable incident. There's something flat and mechanical about it all. Look, for instance, at his use of bland, colourless adjectives: 'powerful', 'silent', 'close', 'great', 'whole', 'slow'.

Seemingly clumsy repetitions continue:

- 'massive' is used twice in quick succession when it would have been easy to select a synonym. It is also recycled later in the poem
- words such as 'pile', 'swinging', 'say', 'water', 'tired' are also repeated
- 'men' is employed three times in very close proximity: 'even the men'; 'very powerful men'; '...silent men'

- the empty intensifier 'very', the sort of word one is told never to use in poetry, is employed in a way that deliberately draws our attention: 'very powerful men/ very ruminative'.

Motion has written about aiming to make the language of his poem's 'as clear as water'. Certainly, the language in this poem appears straightforward, literal, transparent.

And this seems a dangerous strategy – the wattage of the poem is turned down so low that we might be tempted not to bother reading on or to read deeper. If we were judge a poem by its number of striking or memorable lines, we wouldn't judge this one very highly.

The narrator's language is, however, clearly educated: He uses words such as 'nevertheless', 'ruminative', 'trajectory' and 'eclipse'. His social class is also signalled through his reference to a gob of spit as a 'bolus' and to one of the men as a 'fellow'. There is a marked contrast between the inactive observer and silent working men he watches and comments upon. They are men of action; he is a thoughtful, reflective sort of chap. The masculine physicality of the men is emphasised; they are 'massive', 'strong', 'heavy'. However, though observer and

observed seem to have little in common they are both left in the air at the end of the poem, unable to complete whatever they are each doing.

3.
Look, no tricks
Nothing much actually happens in the poem and there is nothing much of great interest that is happening within the prosaic language of the poem. And nothing much is being said in the scene depicted either. It's a virtual dumb show. This is emphasised through repetition: 'silent men'; 'speech was not

something to interest them'; 'still saying nothing', 'no one spoke'. So, at the heart of the poem is silence as well as inaction, another sort of stasis and suspense. There's something postmodern going on here, as if the poem's inside out. It's also an inside out kind of journal - conventionally journals record significant events, when something happens. This journal records an incident where nothing much seems to happen.

In Samuel Beckett's play **Waiting for Godot** (depicted above) the playwright made inaction the central action. Famously nothing happens in *Waiting for Godot*, twice – once in the first half and once in the second. Two tramps wait for the eponymous Godot to arrive, which, of course, he never does. Similarly, the composer John Cage's *'4'3"'* comprises four and a half minutes of silence. At a performance of this piece musicians sit on stage, tune up and then play nothing at all. It is the silence the audience listen to. Or rather they listen to the noises that fill the silence and this comprises the piece's music.

In Motion's poem characters gather, as if for a play, equipment hangs ready in place, the poem's narrator forms an audience; silence and stillness fall. And then nothing happens. However, whereas Cage's piece sensitises an audience to every sound, making them conscious of the act of listening itself, no analogous pay-off on the act of reading is achieved in Motion's poem. We are, perhaps, made conscious of the role of narrating through the repetition of phrases that foreground this role; 'no one said what they saw'; 'I cannot say what'; 'I should say'; 'silent on the subject'. And that seems to be it.

4.

<u>What then is the point of this poem, if indeed a poem needs a point</u>? Well, it appears to me to be a kind of loose extended metaphor for the experience of writer's block. It's not as specific as an allegory, but there's a correspondence between the elements of this narrative and the process of writing a poem:

- the powerful men, the agents who could make this happen, are analogous to the forces of the intellect
- the equipment of chains, hawser and so forth analogous to the resources of language
- the puzzling over a great difficulty equals the struggle to write
- the silence suggests a concentrated state of mind, but also blankness
- the new pile, hanging mid-air is an analogue for the poem itself.

Read this way, the neat trick of the poem is turn the inability to write, the writer's block and its attendant silence, stasis and suspension, into its own subject. Ironically then, not being able to write becomes the subject of writing.

This explanation also helps, arguably, to account for the otherwise incongruous references to the men as 'monsters', to the foreman's 'majesty' and to the hyperbolic sounding 'crack of doom'. If we accept the writing block analogy, then these words express the poet's intense, difficult feelings about writing. Similarly, in this light, the line 'tired, so tired of the whole business' expresses the poet's frustration with what in **East Coker** T. S. Eliot called 'the intolerable wrestle/ with words and meanings'. Andrew Motion has said that his 'poems are the product of a relationship between a side of my mind which is conscious, alert, educated and manipulative, and a side which is as murky as a primeval swamp. I can't predict when this relationship will flower. If I try to goad it into existence I merely engage with one side of my mind or the other, and the poem suffers.' Applying this, we suggest *From the Journal...* dramatises the failed attempt of the conscious, educated side of the poet's mind to access, connect and engage with the mysterious murkiness of his subconscious inner swamp.

From the Journal... crunched

DISCOVERED – PARAPHENALIA – CRANES – PILE – OVER – MASSIVE – POWERFUL – SILENT – SPEECH – IF – MONOSYLLABLES – NEVERTHELESS – OBSCURE – EDGE – STRENGTH – DIFFICULTY – CANNOT – SILENT – REALISED – TIRED – NOTHING – STRONG – CARED – DOOM – SHOULD – JUSTICE – SECRET – CEASED – ABANDONED – POSITION – MYSTIC – NO-ONE – FELLOW – BOLUS – TOBACCO – DESCENT – FOREMAN – TENSION – MAJESTY – AWAY – ECLIPSE – CLOSED – FOLLOWED – MID-AIR

A literary academic, influential poetry editor, ex poet laureate and biographer of Philip Larkin, Andrew Motion is strongly associated with The Movement and its aesthetics. ***From the Journal of a Disappointed Man*** has many characteristics that connect the poem with The Movement style: There's the neat, conventional arrangement of stanzas into regular quatrains; the use of ordinary, pared down 'real' language to describe a real experience; there's the characteristic poet in the role of wry ironic observer of modern life. Motion has, however, updated the aesthetic by being more self-conscious about the act of narrating. He's created a character of the 'disappointed man' who is like a version of a Movement poet, but at one, ironic, self-reflexive remove from the poet himself. In terms of the other poems in the Forward anthology, stylistically there's common ground with Barber's **Material** and Dunmore's **To My Nine-Year-Old Self**. The liminal inbetweeness links the poem to *Copus' An Easy Passage*. An interesting and sophisticated comparison could be made with **Out of the Bag**. In Heaney's poem inspiration springs from encounters with external, mythical or sublime forces - the equivalent of Motion's encounter with something 'primeval'. In Motion's poem, though all the apparatus is assembled encounter is missing, yet the poem is still completed. Mostly this comparison would work through productive contrast.

Daljit Nagra: *look we have coming to Dover!*

1.

Beware the intolerant Daily Mail reader! Beware the grammatical pedant! This poem is going to make you feel quite queasy indeed... Daljit Nagra is an English poet from a Punjabi heritage who uses the unfamiliar Punjabi patois to animate the soundscapes of his poems. Thematically, he is sensitive to both the plurality and duality of his Englishness, where he highlights the struggle to reconcile concepts of England and India as well as inside and outside. **Look we have coming to Dover!** however rewinds time to when his parents and countless others sailed to England in hope of a life 'so various, so beautiful, so new...' to quote Nagra's quotation of the Victorian poet, Matthew Arnold, author of **Dover Beach**. Unusually, for Nagra, this poem is not one that captures the dialectical colour of his Punjabi heritage (check out his reading of his poem **Darling & Me!** on his website).

At present as the UK agonises about migrants and refugees potentially draining the life force out of the country, this poem becomes even more relevant than when first published in 2004. The poem certainly will not ease such agonizing as it plays up to a certain view of economic migrants as projected by conservative, right wing politics. It is a curious poem that seems to simultaneously look inwards and outwards, not an easy feat to achieve.

2.

What's in a title? What's in a subtitle?

A good way to dive into this poem is to fragment it into pieces. Group the most memorable descriptions of place; effective descriptions of reproduction and multiplication and descriptions of brazen conspicuous success. Put your class into groups and ask them to come up with a title based on the fragments they've been given. Then ask them for a subtitle. You could make it challenging for them by asking them to link it to another poem of their choice. If this was too much of a stretch you could furnish them with a few potential candidates! Maybe throw in *Dover Beach* for good measure. Now get them to look at the sets of fragments as one entire text and see what they come up with.

It is doubtful they will arrive at a title like *Look we have coming to Dover!* Typical of the duality of the poem, this title can be interpreted in two ways, resulting in quite divergent tones. Unsurprisingly, perspective is the key. If viewed through the eyes of a grammatical stickler then such an exclamation reveals ignorance and poor mastery of English. If viewed through the eyes of a migrant then such a grasp of the language allows clear communication. It may also reveal pride in the readiness for such a new life. For the reader, whom it can only be hoped is more neutral in perspective, it reveals an almost comic entry into the poem. There is something sweetly amusing about the grammatical fallings of this exciting glimpse of a new world. Regardless of perspective, what the title does is to privilege and prioritise the migrant voice. This is most definitely the voice of the outsider coming in. It is an enthused, innocent voice.

The subtitle's intertextual allusion to *Dover Beach* has a complex effect. On one level it reveals the huge excitement of what awaits these migrants as Dover and all it symbolizes comes into view; hence providing thematic support for that first eager exclamation. However, this new voice is distinctly English, an educated voice that diverges from the initial migrant voice in its precise mastery of the English language. It is the upper middle class voice of the impressive and rather serious looking fellow in the picture, Matthew Arnold. Therefore, Nagra presents a clash of voices before the poem even really begins, which introduces subtly the duality at the heart of the poem. Furthermore, the quotation from *Dover Beach* has been twisted out of its original tonal context. It comes from the end of Arnold's poem where he locates his existential pain in the discrepancy between the beauty of the world as it should be and its chaotic reality. Here Nagra suppresses the chaotic loneliness but keeps the wonder. In another way, this mimics the natural coping mechanism of any migrant travelling to a new, potentially unwelcoming place: stay positive, ignore any negatives!

3.
Welcome to the new old familiar world: sensory overload

Nagra's poem is a sensory barrage for migrant and reader. Unsurprisingly, the first two stanzas are the most sensually overwhelming, with visual, auditory, tactile as well as olfactory imagery. This overload is skilfully twisted to create a hostile physical environment; a development that undermines the chirpy naivety of the poem's title. It is notable how the migrants 'stowed' away on board are confronted with the 'lash of a diesel-breeze'. Here the aggressive onomatopoeia of 'lash' overwhelms the gentle connotations of 'breeze'. Not only does this tactile image suggest hostility in the natural environment to their arrival it also creates uncomfortable connotations with whips, slaves and masters. Furthermore, Nagra uses sibilance that mimics the sound of the sea and the 'lash' of the wind: 's̲towed in the s̲ea to invade / the alfres̲co las̲h.' While Britain's colonial past is summoned cleverly in this image, it also heightens the sensory assault through the olfactory queasiness of a 'diesel-breeze'.

This queasiness is further developed through the 'ratcheting speed into the tide', where the physical movement of the boat through the sea is clearly not designed for migrant comfort. Furthermore, in a symbolic sequence the migrants are literally assailed by the 'surf'. However, this tactile imagery is complicated by the language used. The migrants are besieged by 'gobfuls of surf phlegmed' by rich tourists 'lording the ministered waves'. The position of these 'cushy come-and-go' types is predictably at the front of the boat. Nagra puns nicely on this by describing them as 'prow'd' allowing an unpleasant vanity to characterize these rich people. More worryingly, the conflation of the sea and the rich passengers suggests that the potential xenophobia the migrants might face on the mainland is widespread.

This negative feeling is enhanced in the second stanza where a new sense is introduced: sound. Two significant sounds animate this stanza as the excitement of the initial glimpse of the cliffs gives way to something much more anxiety inducing. The seagulls bring an auditory element to the sensory assault faced by the migrants. Nagra describes them as 'vexing their blarnies'. The verb 'vexing' signals an angry tone and the noun 'blarnies' alludes to the incomprehensibility of the natives they will soon encounter. The symbolism of the 'thunder' adds a further note of menace to their impending arrival. The fact that it 'unbladders /yobbish rain and wind' down on them symbolically prepares them for the storm of indigenous reaction that may await them. The storm literally pisses down on top of them and the adjective 'yobbish' possesses depressing connotations of skinheads and BNP or National Front fanatics. It is no surprise then that the glowing white cliffs first sighted, symbolising hope and new beginnings, have now become a 'vast crumble of scummed/cliffs'. Naive enthusiasm is being squashed by harsh reality.

4.

Presentation of the newcomers: pestilence to residents

This emphasis on the potentially volatile and violent reaction to their arrival is achieved cleverly by blurring perspectives. While the poem is clearly from the perspective of the migrant [look at the various first person pronouns 'I' and 'we'] the language used to describe them is most definitely not language they would use themselves. Rather it is the language of the native, who spies a potentially troublesome newcomer.

This first indication of uneasiness begins when their arrival is described by the verb 'invade'. This military term connotes both an unwanted arrival as well as an inevitable cultural conflict. Other verbs are similarly revealing: The verb 'stowed' conjures up ideas of stowaways, figures who should not be travelling but who ultimately are. In the second stanza, not only does the British sky literally piss down on them they are described as 'hutched in a Bedford van'; the unusual verb 'hutched' is associated with the storage of rabbits and suggests that not only are the migrants animalistic, they are also highly reproductive.

Anxiety about unwanted cultural aliens is played upon expertly by Nagra for the remainder of the poem. This hyperproductivity of rabbits is developed further in the third stanza where the migrants lurking in our midst are 'teemed for breathing', a phrase that puns cleverly to suggest 'teamed for breeding' – every xenophobe's worst nightmare! Not only do they seem to be as plentiful as the 'sweeps of grass' in the park, their power is visualized in their 'poling sparks from pylon to pylon', a striking image that sees the migrants infiltrate the very energy systems of the country. Worryingly, this implies a parasitic strengthening at the expense of the indigenous population. Look at the extended horticultural conceit of grafting in the fourth stanza, where 'swarms' of migrants graft themselves unnoticed onto the host nation, eventually gaining the strength to move 'barefaced' into 'the clear'. The adjective 'barefaced' connotes arrogance, which carries with it the appalled indignation of the white Little Englander. The language used in these stanzas suggests an infestation spreading unnoticed under our noses, one that will only make itself known when it cannot be reversed.

The dominance of visual imagery is surely no coincidence in the final stanza. The migrants transition from hiding in 'the black', 'unclocked by the national eye', to boldly instructing the reader to 'imagine' them luxuriating in wealth. There is a provocative tone of antagonism in the description of the migrants 'Blair'd in cash' where they are 'free' from restraint in their conspicuous enjoyment of wealth. Again Nagra's punning suggests a loud, conspicuous enjoyment of their success through 'Blair'd' echoing 'blared'. The image of these self-made migrants toasting both their own success and their cultural origins in the 'East' can be read as a condemnation or as a celebration. I assume that it is a celebration, but it is elastic enough to recognize a contrary response and allow both to exist side by side.

5.

Speaking in foreign: noise in the poem

A final auditory image of 'babbling ... lingoes' reconnects with the 'vexed blarnies' of the second stanza. But, significantly, in this case it is the migrants who make the noise rather than having to listen to it. Ultimately, Nagra ends his poem with a powerful visual image of the migrants 'flecked by the chalk of Britannia!' A mixing of cultures is signalled, but one where their original Indian heritage is very much in the ascendant. The fricative harshness of being 'flecked by the chalk of Britannia' implies that this is not a harmonious process; rather it is a state reached through tribulation, through cultural conflict. The sharp fricative of the –ck further enhances the unsettling

moment of their cultural revelation. Could it be that the triumphant, almost boastful, success of the migrants at the end of the poem has been learned from the self-assumed superiority of their ex-colonial overlords? It would be tempting to think so, an irony that would no doubt be lost on Little Englanders.

While auditory imagery is a way of illustrating the journey from silent, enduring anxiety to a more confident self-actualisation, the words of the poem itself are also rich in their sound patterns. For example, the memorable alliteration of the moment when the migrants step confidently into the open is located in the last line of the penultimate stanza; they are now 'human' enough to 'hoick' themselves 'bare-faced' into the clear. Again, this suggests they weren't human prior to this, according with the animalistic language used to describe them previously. The verb 'hoick' connects to the grafting/growing conceit in the stanza but can also mean to spit, which is much more provocative. Combined with the strong assonantal spondee of 'bare-faced' this is a sonically powerful moment in the poem, thus reflecting the important evolution in the migrants' cultural self-confidence. Each stanza has its own distinctive sound patterning yet the most important aspect of Nagra's carefully constructed soundscape is that his sound patterns are most pronounced in the final stanza – where the migrants are finally brave enough to find their own voice.

6.

Poetic pace
'Look…!' is a poem virtually tripping over itself in its early stages. The first three stanzas are characterized by a quick poetic pace where enjambment abounds. The first two stanzas essentially have enjambment in every line. A hectic, breathless pace is thus created that is countered by the sensual overload of the description. This makes sense as it mimics the struggle to take in every sensual detail of the new world of Britain in the rush of arrival. Combined with the form, which makes each stanza a sand-alone unit [note the emphatic full stop!], the first two stanzas specifically record the physicality of the place which will now be home. Each stanza almost represents one huge intake of breath followed by a frantic recounting of the barrage of sensory experience confronting these long travelling migrants.

However, this sense of excited observation begins to slow towards the end of the poem. The final stanza only has two examples of enjambment, which imposes a statelier pace. In the context of the overall narrative trajectory of the poem this is apposite; the migrants have now established themselves in their new home. Now 'Blair'd in cash' they are confident and conspicuous as they emerge from their initial anxious desires to blend into the background, hiding 'in / the black within shot of the moon's / spotlight'.

7.

Wave form

Nagra has shaped his poem into five regular looking five line stanzas, or cinquains. Roughly speaking, his stanzas have a short opening line [5 to 7 syllables] followed by three longer lines [mostly 10 to 12 syllables] and a final line, which is the longest [14 or 15 syllables]. There is no rhyme scheme and the metre while full of strong beats is unpredictable and essentially free verse. <u>So why does he impose such a visually rigid form on this unpredictable, high paced torrent of description?</u>

While the regular rigidity of the form contrasts markedly with the irregularity of the poetic content, it is visually distinct and invites analysis. In one sense the form of the stanzas mimics the growth in numbers as well as cultural strength of the migrants. In a term favoured by alarmists there is a clear 'wave'-like aspect to the form. Each stanza looks like a wave coming closer and closer up the shore before retreating to start all over again (a device that mirrors, but adapts, the form of Arnold's *Dover Beach*). While this connects clearly to the journey by sea, it also links to the concept of cycles, in this case cycles of human migration from the developing world to the West. Another more out-there interpretation of the form provides us with five cinquains or five by five, a term used in radio communication to rate the loudness and the clarity of a radio signal. Applying this to the poem, the voice of the migrants has grown from silent anonymity to a voice that is loud and clear.

In summary, Nagra's poem plays on racist stereotyping of immigrants, using this knowingly and satirically. An innocent immigrant enthusiasm for England is confronted by the experience of xenophobic hostility and ugly weather. But the poem ends happily, at least, for the immigrants, safely prosperous.

Come we make good crunching now!

STOWED – LASH – BRUNT – PHLEGMED – PROW'D – SEAGULL – BLARNIES – CRUMBLE – UNBLADDERS – HUTCHED – REAP – NATIONAL – TEEMED – SWEEPS – ENNOBLED – SWARMS – BLACK – MIRACLE – PASSPORT – BARE-FACED – IMAGINE – BLAIR'D – FREE – RAISE – LINGOES

The innocence and experience narrative arc of ***Look we have coming to Dover!*** links it to poems such as Copus' ***An Easy Passage*** and Dunmore's ***To My Nine-Year-Old Self***. The poem's setting and innovative use of form would make an interesting comparison with Burnside's ***History***, while the theme of identity and place link Nagra's poem to Heaney's ***Out of the Bag***. Finally, the satirical take on modern could be compared to O'Driscoll's ***Please Hold*** or Turnbull's ***Ode to a Grayson Perry Urn***.

Ciaran O'Driscoll, *please hold*

1.

The scream

Norwegian artist, Edvard Munch's Expressionist painting *The Scream* is

probably the most iconic image of angst and alienation. Completed in 1883, the painting depicts an androgynous figure with a skull-like head crossing a bridge towards us, screaming. Whereas Impressionist painters tried to capture transient external reality, Expressionists sought to convey their own intense feelings, projecting these onto their canvases. Here it is as if the character's scream echoes through and is converted visually into an intense swirling landscape. Google the image and you'll see that the correspondence between screaming individual and screaming landscape is signalled by the shared colours and sinuous shapes. It's as if the entire natural world has become a scream.

What does O'Driscoll's poem have in common with Munch's painting?

In **Please Hold** the narrator experiences similar feelings of alienation and entrapment and, of course, he ends up screaming. O'Driscoll's poem dramatises a theme that is perhaps the most common in all literature and art - the often fraught relationship between the individual and society. Where the cause of the screaming in Munch's painting is not obvious, in *Please Hold*, as in some dystopian sci-fi, the trauma comes from interaction with the faceless authority of a machine.

2.

Alternative facts

Though the poem is undoubtedly comic and the situation the narrator finds himself is presented as being absurd, it has serious points too. Real human communication is here being replaced by automated systems, supposedly in the name of efficiency. But, as anyone who has ever had the misfortune of spending time locked into one of these sorts of circular interactions with an automated answering machine will know too well, often the time-devouring, temper-testing experience is far from efficient. Moreover, there is a loss of proper human interaction. Though it might mimic some of the features of human conversation, such as turn-taking, this conversation is a fake. Despite all the options on offer, the interaction also fails its basic purpose; to address the narrator's actual 'needs'. Furthermore, some cultural commentators, such as the radical economist Charles Eisenstein, argue that the sort of corporate lying inherent in this wearingly familiar aspect of modern life is actually damaging and dangerous. Over time universally used untruths, such as the fake friendliness of 'your call is important to us', degrade the quality of our communication and erode our ability to distinguish truth from lies, making us all more vulnerable to manipulation. Or so they argue.

3.

Dead language

Stylistically, with its ironic relocation of the colourless functional language of officialese into the lyric world of poetry, O'Driscoll's *Please Hold* is related to poems such as Henry Reed's WWII poem **Naming of Parts**, Peter Porter's

Your Attention Please and Simon Armitage's *Hand Washing Technique –
Government Guidelines*. In his poem, Reed ironically contrasts the stark,
flat, euphemistic language of the military with sonorous imagery describing
nature. As a recruit is instructed how to assemble a gun - 'this you can see is
the bolt. The purpose of this/ Is to open the breech, as you see. We can slide
it/ Rapidly backwards and forwards...' his mind wanders onto the beauty of
nature, expressed in romantic mode:

'The branches/ hold in the gardens their silent, eloquent gestures.'

Porter's poem imitates the bland language of a public information broadcast;
the terrifying idea of a nuclear attack and inevitable annihilation is related
through unemotional and practical sounding, but hopelessly inadequate,
instructions. A response to the enquiry into the apparent suicide of the arms
expert and UN weapons inspector David Kelly in 2003, Armitage's poem
ironically applies government advice on handwashing to this context. A found
poem, such as Armitage's, is made of language discovered in any non-poetic
context and then re-presented as a poem. While Reed's, Porter's and
O'Driscoll's are not strictly found poems, they all use language as if verbatim,
drawn from about the most distinctly non-poetic contexts conceivable.

The language in O'Driscoll's poem is, for example, devoid of metaphors or
other types of figurative imagery, such as symbolism or personification. Nor
are there any instances of the other form of imagery, sensory. Sensory
imagery is evocative; it helps us to visualise, hear and feel the words of a
poem, forging connections between us and the experiences described.
O'Driscoll's poem is entirely stripped of sensory imagery. Mostly composed of
dull, prosaic function words, the poem also features very few adjectives. The
ones it does include, such as 'great' and 'wonderful' are colourless and
emptied, in this context, entirely of meaning. Language can be simple, literal,
pared-down and yet still beautiful. The language *in Please Hold*, however, is
deliberately flat, lumpen, graceless and ugly.

Elegant variation is a writing principle that underpins a lot of stylish writing. In a nutshell, it means avoiding repetition of words, phrases, syntax, punctuation and sentence lengths, unless doing so serves a specific purpose. O'Driscoll artfully ignores this principle so that his poem is full of clumsy and grating repetition:

- on a word level, lots of words are repeated when synonyms could easily have been found: 'future', 'wife', 'giving', 'when', 'number', 'wonderful', 'great', 'account', 'money', 'options', 'nothing', 'says', 'please', 'hold', 'robot', 'means', 'grow' and so forth. Often, they are repeated close together, sometimes in succeeding lines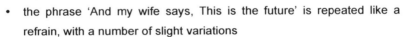
- often these repeated words also appear in the same position in a line. The word 'number', for instance, appears at the end of line 8, 10, 11 and 12, whereas nine lines start with 'and'
- phrases are also repeated: 'my wife says', 'please hold', 'says the robot', 'you can say' etc.
- the phrase 'And my wife says, This is the future' is repeated like a refrain, with a number of slight variations
- groups of lines are also repeated, such as the first three. About two thirds of the way through the line 'and I'm talking to a robot on the phone' is reused, implying we have are back to start and the 'conversation' has gone precisely nowhere
- the syntax of many of the lines is strikingly similar: subject, verb, object
- many of the sentences are of a similar length
- full stops and commas litter the poem, only relieved by one set of brackets and one exclamation mark!
- typically the sentences are declaratives, statements rather than descriptions. Declarative sentence follows declarative statement with very little change or relief

- some lines and sentences start and end in the same way, giving the impression that there has been no progress or movement. The best examples of this circularity are the poem's first three lines which start and end with 'future says...' The last stanza also opens and closes with the phrase 'Please hold'. The first thing we read, the title, *Please Hold* is also the last: The phrase preceding this 'This is the future' was also the first line. So, like the narrator, the reader has been caught up in an enormous, closed loop. Even at the end of the poem we haven't reached any conclusion or end point; the last thing we read is 'please hold'. In this way, the present and the future collapse into each other and become indistinguishable in the poem; literally we are going around in circles, getting nowhere.

In neat mimicry of the laborious automated answering service, we've established that the poem is jam-packed full of clumsily, inelegantly, repetitive, dull, soulless language which loops back, entrapping itself. With all those commas and full stops, bereft of the underpinning spring of metre, it's also rhythmically ugly, choppy, lumpy and flat. The poem's lines move awkwardly, in jagged fits and starts; there is no flow or elasticity to the language, as there would be in real human conversation.

So, what's the effect of this all-pervasive repetition?

Clearly it conveys the spirit-sapping poverty of the (mis)communication that's taking place, the degrading of real human experience. Simple language should at least make the transaction quick and simple. In fact, it does nothing

of the sort, because this is not a proper two-way conversation. It also makes the reader feel what the poem's narrator feels – trapped in an inauthentic 'conversation' that is going nowhere and going there excruciatingly slowly. This is a modern sort of hell. Because, as well as the functional language of the answering machine being unpoetic, it is also blatantly insincere, and that just adds insult to the injury. Presumably, for example, the answering machine is not in a position to judge whether the narrator's phone number is or is not 'wonderful'. As the narrator sarcastically observes 'I have a wonderful telephone number'. If it is not an evaluation of the quality of the number, the 'wonderful' most refer to the fact that the narrator has provided his number, something unlikely to be labelled as 'wonderful' by any real or sane person. The same goes for the abuse of the word 'great'. The reason for using an automated service is not, in fact, to make the experience as straightforward and painless as possible for the user, but to save the money, the cost of paying a real person to take the call. Hence phrases such as 'we appreciate your patience' and 'your call is important to us' are blatantly untrue and part of what drives the narrator into such a frenzy of impotent rage.

4.

Dystopia now!

O'Driscoll's poem paints a bleak picture of the present/future in which potentially rich human interactions are supplanted by human to machine ones. Interestingly, the poet consistently refers to an automated service as a robot and as a 'he'. 'Robot' has distinctly Sci-fi connotations that automated answering service does not. In Sci-fi dystopias, such as the *Terminator* films the machines are taking over and aim to crush all human resistance. In *Please Hold* the machines do not rise up and conquer mankind with superior intelligence and high-tech weaponry. Instead this robot drives its human interlocutor to the point of distraction, wasting his life and vanquishing his spirit. Quite an effective tactic, in fact.

This is a comic poem. It presents an absurd situation: We have, for instance, a 'mind-reading robot'; when the man says he will be driven to looting, the robot's response is 'wonderful', and after the musical interlude the man discovers that the robot transfers him back to itself. And so on. Moreover, the narrator's escalating frustration and impotency, in contrast to the robot's unchanging blankness, is painfully entertaining (for us). But, as the final, separate stanza makes clear, there's a serious issue too. The poet implies that there's an element of deliberate control underlying the apparently helpful use of an automated service: 'please do what you're told'. After all, these interactions can only follow a predetermined pattern, fixed by the 'service provider'. It's not possible to get into an argument you can win with an automated service, there's no chance to complain or make a case or change the nature of the exchange. This fixedness denies the human a voice and disempowers him, reduces the narrator to passively following instructions. The robot has all the power.

What of the overall form of the poem? Apart from the final tercet it's one unremitting block of language, a wall of words against which the poet and reader can bang their heads, repeatedly.

Crunching *Please Hold* further highlights the repetitiveness of the poem's diction.

FUTURE – SAME – PRESENT – ROBOT – OPTIONS – NEEDS – WONDERFUL – NUMBER – GREAT – NUMBER – NUMBER – NUMBER – NOTHING – TELEPHONE – REALLY – MONEY – NOTHING – FREE - SHOUT – WONDERFUL – GREAT – WONDERFUL – FUTURE – UNDERSTAND – SAY – SAY – CAN – ROBOTIC – SCREAM – FUTURE – SAME – PRESENT – ROBOT – OPTIONS – GUISE – APPRECIATE – HOLD – HOLD – FUCKING – HIMSELF – IMPORTANT – MEANS – NOT – FUTURE – HOLD – MEANS – NEEDS – LOOTING – COLD – TOLD – HOLD.

With its comic/ serious satirical take on modern culture, *__Please Hold,__* **could be compared with** *One to a Grayson Perry Urn, From the Journal of a Disappointed Man* **and** *Chainsaw versus the Pampas Grass.*

Adam Thorpe, *On Her Blindness*

1.

When is chopped up prose just chopped up prose and when can it be seen to clamber to the airy heights of poetry? It's a tough call for sure and novelist Adam Thorpe sails close to the wind with this free verse poem that seems to rather arbitrarily cut 17 sentences into 22 couplets and one poetically lonely line. Additionally, it also seems more like a mini-prose narrative with its collection of anecdotal observations and corresponding personal contemplations. Can clever lineation alone lift carefully arranged prose into poetry? I'm doubtful. There must be an intensity of expression, a boldness of imaginative description and a deep core of emotional profundity that rescues poetry from being merely prosaic.

Luckily, Thorpe explores loss at the uncomfortably close distance of 'a fortnight back'. Above all else it is the lack of emotional distance from the traumatic event the poem narrates that transforms his prose into poetry. Deeply personal, and consequently deeply universal, the loss of a parent awaits us all. Like the majority of such losses, the loss here is not a serene death due to natural circumstances during sleep, but a long drawn out process of deterioration, defiance and dependence.

Comprising 22 regular couplets, superficially the poem seems composed, neat and orderly. Beneath this outer composure, however, is a striking internal disorder. The regular holding outer pattern of the couplet is, in fact, under considerable internal stress. Unmetred, the form is like cut-up prose, especially in the proliferation of enjambment that characterises almost every couplet and the inevitably high number of caesuras that such enjambment creates. A combination of fast pace and stuttering pauses adds to an impression of underlying emotional turmoil. Notice how the poignancy of the ending is amplified by the loss of a poetic line in what should be the concluding couplet, a loss that mirrors the actual loss of Thorpe's mother

2.

The blind leading the not-blind

On Her Blindness through its title reaches backwards through time to John Milton's *When I Consider How My Light Is Spent (On His Blindness)* a poem that voices the helplessness of the blind from the perspective of the blind. Crucially, Thorpe changes this perspective to those who watch the blind from the outside, who spectate on their helplessness. In an odd way this intensifies the feelings of helplessness that drive the poem. It is the contrast between the 'inadequate [...] locked-in son' and the woman who somehow 'kept her dignity' that is so striking.

It is the mother's active, stoical defiance of her 'catastrophic / handicap' that the poem promotes. Thorpe employs an almost black humour in his capturing of her plight. She is described 'bumping into cars like a dodgem', she insists

on driving 'the old Lanchester /long after it was safe' and perhaps most pathetically, she 'admires' films and television /while looking the wrong way.' There is something noble about how 'she pretended to ignore /the void; or laughed it off.' Indeed, the overall poetic message seems to advocate a healthy dose of

humour in warding off the annihilating darkness of her disability. However, this is not to say that Thorpe does not treat his subject with the seriousness it deserves. He employs a molussus [and ear hooking alliteration] at the start of the 'long /slow slide had finished in a vision /as blank as stone,' which endows his topic with a befitting sonic gravity. The poet also combines this metrical power with his most effective piece of figurative language to ensure that the deft balance of tragic-comedy stays firmly in tragic waters. The 'blank as stone' simile foregrounds the dehumanising debilitation of his mother's illness and also its complete invincibility. The simile also captures something of the calcifying processes that turn her from the 'bumping [...] dodgem' to 'too weak to move'.

In contrast, the poet's own passivity and powerlessness renders him more pathetic than the mother who tells him frankly she 'could not bear being blind' (one of the most memorably alliterative moments in the poem). Whereas the pretence she develops in public seems admirable in its usage as a coping strategy, his inability to say nothing or nothing of use renders him impotent, an unwilling spectator in an unwanted theatre of cruelty. His mortifying faux pas of raving about 'the autumn trees around the hospital /ablaze with colour' to his blind dying mother is searingly honest and again, darkly comic. Such awkward moments capture the reality of how 'inadequate' non-sufferers actually are for those who suffer illnesses that strip away taken-for-granted humanity.

3.

Seeing is pretending

However, the poem, while ending in a poignant finality, offers a shred (and I think it could only be that) of hope. The gift for pretence has been bequeathed from the dead to the living. Now, rather than his mother pretending it is 'up to us to believe /she was watching, somewhere, in the end'. In the same way that his mother memorably pretended to like his kids' 'latest drawing, or [...] new toy' as a way of making every day bearable, her mourners are encouraged to pretend to see her in a new light, to bear the burden of her loss. The poem attempts to understand the anguish of the 'living hell' his mother felt in a way that is naive, yet cathartic.

The pretending is signalled by the key verb 'believe', which gives this pretence a distinctly religious tone. To believe that the dearly departed are 'watching, somewhere, in the end' suggests a belief in an afterlife where Thorpe's mother is restored to her full powers. The caesuras surrounding 'somewhere' in the final line alter its potential meaning from 'she was watching somewhere' in the distance (i.e. gazing serenely into the distance) to 'she was watching somewhere' different (i.e. she is watching us from a different place). There is also the comic possibility, which would be disrespectful if not for the aforementioned comic treatment of his mother's disability, of her finally allowed 'to sink into television /while looking the [right] way'. Regardless, this emphasis on pretence as a coping strategy places the emphasis on the coping part rather than the pretence part. Religious beliefs can be dismissed as misguided, naive self-delusion by atheists, but should also be recognised as an imaginative coping strategy for the harshness of life; a coping method no less imaginative or consoling than the best literature has to offer.

4.
Afterglow or aftermath?
Hopefully, it is now apparent how conflicted this poem is in its treatment of its chosen topic – it constantly teeters on the brink of collapse, somehow traversing the boundaries between poetry and prose, tragedy and comedy, order and disorder, the trivial and the profound in a memorably awkward yet admirable manner.

Nowhere is this more painfully acute than in Thorpe's beautiful evocation of his mother's death, nestled symbolically in the bosom of nature's beauty – a beauty that is absolutely of no consolation to his blind mother. There is something moving about the idealised 'autumn trees around the hospital /ablaze with colour' that brings so much consolation to him rather than his mother. Again, the dark comedy of his vibrant evocation of nature's beauty for his blind mother being both futile and noble embodies the crux of the problem: how do you pretend to understand something you have not experienced yourself?

Again, it seems that success in this regard is ultimately irrelevant – it is the trying to console that is more important; generosity of spirit to at least try to empathise can be enough in itself. Regardless, the setting of 'the ground royal /with leaf-fall' bestows a dignity on his mother's death that is appropriate for a woman who 'kept her dignity'. How much of an artistic pretence this is remains to be seen, but it is fitting that she departs into the metaphorical darkness 'ablaze with colour'. It reflects the vibrant strategies of affectation that his mother employed so effectively.

On Her Blindness crunched

BLIND – SHOULDN'T – CATASTROPHIC – HANDICAPS – BEAR – JOY – FIGHT – RESTAURANT – FORK – TRY – WHISPERED – HELL – HOPE – RECALL – SOP – INADEQUATE – DIGNITY – DODGEM – DIRECTION – COMPASS – PRETENDED – LAUGHED – COULDN'T – SHOW – FORGET – SLIDE – BLANK – DRIVE – SAFE – EXHIBITIONS – SINK – WRONG – LAST – GOLDEN – AUTUMN – ABLAZE – LEAF-FALL – STARING – NOTHING – DYING – SIGHTLESS - EYELIDS – COFFIN – WATCHING

A number of poems in the selection explore relationships with mothers and with mortality. Most obviously *Effects*, like *On Her Blindness,* is an elegy exploring both topics together. *Material*, *Out of the Bag* and *Genetics* also spring to mind as potential comparisons.

Tim Turnbull, *Ode on a Grayson Perry Urn*

1.

An interesting way into Turnbull's poem would be to google Grayson Perry's

art and, in particular, the images from his exhibition *The Vanity of Small Things*. In this exhibition, artist and documentary film-maker, Grayson Perry, presents six tapestries depicting the life of a fictional character, Tim Rakewell. Starting with his birth, these intensely brightly coloured, cartoonishly rendered tapestries trace Rakewell's ascent through and across modern Britain, from the Cotswolds to Sunderland. In this way, they present a cross section of modern British culture. Characteristically, Perry's tapestries are intertextual: as titles such as *The Annunciation of the Virgin Deal* indicate, each tapestry draws on and references iconography from famous religious paintings. Echoing the series of paintings by the eighteenth century English artist William Hogarth called *A Rake's Progress*, the narrative of Rakewell is also intertextual. And, the medium itself, tapestry, sets up a series of expectations in terms of content that Perry references and subverts.

In simultaneous dialogue with John Keats's seminal poem *Ode to a Grecian Urn* (1819) and Perry's art works, Turnbull's poem follows a similarly self-consciously intertextual pattern. And, like Perry's work, Turnbull's poem uses

Keats' Ode as an ironic backdrop for a vibrant but garish vision of modern British life. As the poem states, whether this vision is celebratory or condemnatory depends on the eye of the beholder.

John Keats was part of the Romantic movement in poetry, which also included poets such as Wordsworth, Byron and Shelley. The Romantics' poetry is characterised by discussion of nature, and of the palpable sadness at man's inability to reach a true essence of purity and 'oneness' with it. Keats was credited with the reworking of the ode form (a classical Greek poem structure), and similarly, Turnbull makes no apologies for taking Keats' poem and crafting a challenging response.

Keats' poem is a tribute to, and celebration of, classical Greek art- specifically, here, an 'urn' or large vase, upon which pictures are drawn of pastoral Greek life. Keats believed that classical art presented the ideal of Greek virtue and classical life, which is the foundation of the poem. The two scenes that he chooses to narrate are a lover who fruitlessly pursues his beloved, and of some rural villagers in the lead-up to performing a sacrifice. The poem makes an implied contrast between the ideal it depicts and the contemporary world in which Keats lived.

Both poems are about the physicality of 'things', whether this be a neo-classical vase representing antique craft or 'A kitschy vase / some Shirley Temple manqué has knocked out'. Turnbull's dismissive, irreverent description of a mass-produced vase contrasts with Keats' admiration of his elegant, ancient Greek version. <u>What do you think Turnbull is saying by setting up this comparison?</u>

2.

Owed to the ode; adaptation

The most obvious piece of aesthetic, or self-aware 'creation' and artificiality, is in the title. Writers, to some extent, are always adapting previous sources (this goes right down to the very fact that all language must be re-used unless you make up your own words!) However, Turnbull might as well just cite Keats on this; he is deliberately asking the reader to examine what adaptation is and what effect it has on us. Do you think that a direct adaptation makes the writer less legitimate? Is the end work still as accomplished or do you think a writer should be coming up with as new material as possible each time? Why?

Frances Spalding noted an interesting aspect of adaptation whilst talking about Myfanwy Piper's study of Picasso – that '[Picasso's] modernity lay not in the shattering of form, but in the need to find a way of dealing with the remaining fragments... not a new world but the old world in new and shattered circumstances'. Turnbull's poem is in critical dialogue with Keats's and these 'shattered circumstances' are clearly recognisable:

- Keats' question 'What men or gods are these?... What wild ecstasy?' is answered with Turnbull's 'children. They will stay out late /forever, pumped on youth and ecstasy, /on alloy, bass and arrogance'
- Keats' sylvan 'pipes and timbrels' and 'soft pipes' become Turnbull's 'screech of tyres and the nervous squeals /of girls' and 'throb of UK garage'
- Perhaps one of the most direct nods - after the title - that Turnbull makes to the form of Keats' poem is the ending. Whilst Keats' famous closing lines read 'Beauty is truth, truth beauty,- that is all /Ye know on earth, and all ye need to know', Turnbull suggests that, actually, reality is far more fluid and uncertain - 'who knew that truth was all negotiable /and beauty in the gift of the beholder'. Keats's lofty, declarative aphorism is replaced, and undercut, with a relativistic question, couched in everyday speech.

This is also a nod to the construction of the poem itself. The idea that the canon (the types of literature considered important and 'set in stone' for, for example, a syllabus) must be untouched is directly challenged here. The

Romantic poets spent a lot of time thinking about the pure essence of beauty, especially that found in nature, and one argument for the power of their poetry is the constant sadness and distress it evokes from the fact that that pure beauty can never be attained. Perhaps Turnbull is saying that the beauty of Keats' 'original' is in his power - and that it is our gift, as a reader, to be the 'beholder' and make the poem our own. Whilst this doesn't necessarily mean we have to go out and rewrite every classical poem we come across, it does mean that no meaning is fixed - just as Turnbull has reworked a Romantic narrative voice for a modern social context. Hence Turnbull's poem reflects shifts in the concept of the reader in modern literary criticism: Whereas in Keats' time, the writer was seen as the prime controller of meaning, modern criticism, as you'll know from your A-level assessment objectives, argues that the reader is a significant, active maker of meaning. Every reading is, in effect, an act of recreation.

3.
How Romantic are both poems?
The Romantic period is sometimes stereotyped as being about the tempestuous lives of a group of troubled poets. This isn't really an unfair judgement as there was plenty of relationship distress amongst the poets we mentioned earlier. However, there are obviously other very important hallmarks. In particular, there was a major emphasis on the physical experience of nature and of God. Sometimes this was shown in poems like *The Eolian Harp* (Coleridge's study of a harp as a method of attaining a purity of natural experience) and sometimes it was expressed through the violence of physical creation and disorder (a perfect example being Mary Shelley's novel *Frankenstein*, written in 1818).

Turnbull also mirrors this Romantic inclination to connect with the deepest essence of human existence; he does so by bringing out the earthiest and most guttural parts of physicality and sexuality. His language evokes this earthiness all the way through. For example, the growly onomatopoeia of 'throaty turbo roar' reverberates through to 'joyful throb', to 'alloy, bass and arrogance'. The momentum of these 'o' sounds is suddenly stopped with the bright, lighter, but still harsh, 'screech of tyres and the nervous squeals / of girls'. The people 'pumped on youth and ecstasy' even enter their bodies into the horrific sounding 'chlamydia roulette'. It is worth unpicking this striking image: Karl Marx once said that women's bodies were the original form of currency as they were traded for other goods. If it were just money being gambled, we could accuse the characters of superficiality. Instead, bodies are being exchanged in an anarchic marketplace of 'lives so free and bountiful', where everything is 'negotiable' - returning to what Marx claims is the original form of currency, back to the physical roots of all human commerce.

4.

Free bodies

It is obviously also not just women, here, who are being traded. Each girl is 'buff [and] each geezer toned and strong'. Modern British society is depicted

in free-wheeling, vivid, Perry-style technicolour, but the vision is hardly utopian - 'given head /in crude games', 'dead suburban streets', 'rat-boys' and 'crap estates'. Perhaps we should read the poem as a lament for the cheapening and coarsening of popular culture. Indeed, the poem's breezy, colloquial and sometimes coarse idiom - 'knocked out', 'pumped on', 'geezer(s)', 'given head' - stands in stark contrast to Keats' rarefied vocabulary and phrasing. Perhaps, in fact, Turnbull's poem presents a dystopian vision of societal decline.

However, the imagery is as vibrant as it is garish. And just as Keats describes the 'wild ecstasy' of the ancient Greeks, Turnbull also offers a picture of liberation - 'lives so free and bountiful', 'how happy'. Moreover, Turnbull's poem presents a world more liberal and progressive than Keats', one where the connection with our physical existence is far more accessible than the Romantics thought it was. Whereas Keats' 'heart high-sorrowful' yearns for 'all breathing human passion far above', Turnbull's 'human passion' is immediate, touchable, real.

The characters consensually engage in this world within Turnbull's text, unlike the 'heifer lowing at the skies' that is lead to the sacrificial altar in Keats' *Grecian Urn*. Another example of freedom shown in Turnbull's poem is the fact that most lines are not given a hiatus by punctuation; the majority flow freely into the next, with uncapitalised words at the beginnings of lines:

'but these wheels will not lose traction, skid and flip, no harm / befall these children'.

Conversely, Keats' lines are held back by constant commas, question marks and full stops, reigning the passage of language in to mirror the constrained artifice of the urn itself: 'by river or sea shore, / Or mountain-built with peaceful citadel, / Is emptied of this folk, this pious morn? / And...' These lines move hesitantly, sedately, conveying pensive thought, but also uncertainty. In stark contrast, Turnbull's ode is speeded-up, turbo-charged, at full-throttle; the lines rush onwards conveying the pace and energy of modern life.

A useful bit of philosophy to look at here is Thomas Hobbes' **Leviathan**, published in 1651. Hobbes suggested that human beings are just physical objects, and that all of their actions can be explained in purely mechanical terms. Hobbes also says that power only exists where there is a mutual agreement between the ruler and those being ruled, and perhaps most famously that all the different bodies acting in their own interests produce a world where life is 'solitary, poor, nasty, brutish and short'. We have already seen that Turnbull's characters enter their bodies as objects into the narrative's 'roulette'; the poem gives them a short life cycle before catapulting  far into the future, 'millennia hence'. They don't seem to recognise any higher

153

authority, 'too young to quite appreciate / the peril they are in'. Life in this poem certainly seems 'short' and perhaps 'brutish'- but is it really 'nasty' or 'poor'?

Similarly, in terms of the self-reflective debate about the value of art, the poem raises the question of whether something that is variously described as 'kitschy', 'gaudy' and a 'garish crock' (phrases that could be levelled against the poem itself – the elegant, classical form of the Ode stuffed full with gaudy content) can, in fact, be just as beautiful and 'true' as great works from the literary and artistic canons.

5.
Further questions:
Does Turnbull's poem reassure you that life is in front of the reader to be grasped - or does it alienate you with the intensity of description?
How far do you think both poems exaggerate or bend the truth?
Why might they do that?

Ode to a Grayson Perry Urn crunched

KISTCHY – VASE – KIDS – CARS – BEDLAM – FRIGHT – EXPOSE – TURBO – THROB – SQUEALS – YOUTH – ECSTASY – ARROGANCE – URBAN – GIRL – GEEZER – CHLAMYDIA – CHEERLEADERS – PENSIONERS – RICH – GARISH – FREE – HAPPY – TRUTH – BEAUTY

Turnbull emphasises the power involved throughout the process of adaptation. Other poems in the anthology that are in 'dialogue with' other poems, or artworks, include *Look We Have Coming to Dover!*, *On Her Blindness* and *Balaklava*. *Please Hold* is another poem which takes a comic, satirical approach to presenting modern life.

A sonnet of revision activities

1. Top ten poems. Each student ranks the poems in a top ten selection, writing brief reasons for their choices. One student writes their top ten on the whiteboard. Others are then invited to knock one poem out and to move one poem up or down. The aim is to arrive at class consensus

2. Top ten lines – ditto

3. Group the poems according to different aspects, form, theme, tone, language, context. Ideally use a big piece of paper and colouring pens and make as many links as possible

4. Use Venn diagrams to visualise shared details between poems

5. Visualise a poem: Present it as a single picture or diagram that captures its essence

6. Turn it into a storyboard for a film. Think of the transitions between stanzas as different film shots; are they cross-cuts, fades, dissolves? What sort of soundtrack does the film need? What are the ambient sounds? For a brilliant example of a film poem check out *The Black Delph Bride* by Liz Berry: ttps://www.youtube.com/watch?v=JT0izGJCHO8

7. Match the poem with another text. This can be an image, a song, a memory, an extract from a Geography text book, but it has to be something that makes the poem resonate in a new light

8. If the poem were a piece of music what would it be? Which poems are the poetic equivalent of death metal, free form jazz or gangsta rap, which are more like your favourite classical piece?

9. Apply critical theories to the poems. What would a Feminist critic make of Armitage's poem? Why might a Marxist be interested in *Eat Me*? Turn the concise descriptions on different theories in *The Art of Writing English Literature Essays, for A-level and Beyond*, into cards, put a class in pairs with one poem each. They have five minutes to try to apply each card to the poem. Alternatively, all the class examine the same poem but each pair is given a different critical perspective. Discuss findings

10. Write questions to ask each poet about their poem. Swap with another student and try to answer the questions they have written

11. Place the poems on a continuum with radically experimental at one pole and well-made/ conventional/ traditional at the other. Try this task taking the poem as a whole and then try it again, breaking the poems down to their constituent elements of form, language, topic. Some poems, for instance, might be radical in terms of topic but conventional in terms of form. Agbabi's *Eat Me*, for instance, might fall into this category

12. Write sample paragraphs on key aspects of each poem. A paragraph just on figurative imagery, another on the poet's use of sonic devices

13. Write a response to the poem in any form you like. You are the mother in *Material*, the mermaid in *Giuseppe,* Lukas in *History*. Write your thoughts in whatever form you like

14. Play a variation of the popular Radio 4 panel game, *The Unbelievable Truth*. Each student has to write a two minute speech about a poem from the Anthology. During their speech they have to try to smuggle 5 lies about the poem past the rest of the class. The rest of the class have to try to spot these lies.

Critical soundbites

In this demanding revision activity, students have to match the following excerpts from criticism to the poet whose work they describe. (Answers are at the end of this book). In an added twist, two of these soundbites are impostors, either about a poet not in the selection or entirely fictitious. See if you can spot them.

1. Her poems deal with private and communal loss, a theme established by the opening poem...the poet combines elegiac thoughts...with touching memories.

2. The poet's perennial themes are love and loss, the transience of nature and of human lives.

3. 'I love this big-eyed, Frankenstein-like imagining, and the shiver of remembered fear it brings with it.'

4. 'It doesn't matter if it's breath, blood, a drum loop, jazz syncopation, the pentameter or whatever, you gotta get a rhythm, a working rhythm.'

5. The poet, 'enjoys a reputation as a poet consistently sympathetic in' their 'observation of human lives – particularly of' their 'own family's history – as well as the rhythms of social change and the natural world'.

6. Apparently, poet x writes 'witty, markedly contemporary first-person lyrics with a pseudo-confessional edge that revel in what Elizabeth Bishop famously called 'the surrealism of the everyday'; exposing the false distinction between the ordinary and extraordinary through exploring the rich vicissitudes of human experience'.

7. 'It could be said that just as some writers use humour as an antidote to despair' this poet 'uses humour to make expressions of anger more palatable.'

8. 'Perhaps' this poet's 'most significant poetic achievement so far...lies in his ability to deconstruct literary, cultural and social conventions in often darkly comic ways.'

9. Poet y 'populates' their 'work with solitary, outsider figures, sometimes only partly human, stranded on the borders between worlds and excluded from normal human relationships.'

10. 'I want my writing to be as clear as water. No ornate language; very few obvious tricks. I want readers to be able to see all the way down through its surfaces into the swamp. I want them to feel they're in a world they thought they knew, but which turns out to be stranger, more charged, more disturbed than they realised.'

11. 'The ultimate aim of the poet should be to touch our hearts by showing his own, and not to exhibit his learning, or his fine taste, or his skill in mimicking the notes of his predecessors.'

12. Their 'poems are beautifully controlled with a literary sophistication which does not preclude tenderness' their 'poems encompass historical imaginings and domestic scenes, and are appreciative of worldwide cultures'.

13. Their poems try to disentangle past, present and future, yet court situations in which such divisions are blurred.

14. Their poems move from domesticity into the territory of folk tales, Biblical stories, Greek myths, paintings and dreams. Her work is emotional but cunning, and like proverbial Nature, at times red in tooth and claw.

15. Formally elegant, lightly constructed, her poems provocatively explore the sadness and happiness of life – from ancient Rome, Renaissance Italy, revolutionary Paris, to today, we see courage in the face of love and loss, wry humour and acceptance when confronted with sorrow.

16. Dark shadows, childhood traumas, the close presences of the dead, and above all the omnipresence of death throughout life; all these elements recur throughout his poetry

17. Their poems possess a vitality...a heightened chattiness that combines idiomatic cliché with arresting and often unusual observations and descriptions, spanning his favoured territory of tall tales, humorous dramatic monologues and often sinister, noirish anecdotes.

18. Their poetry revels in exploring the complex flux of the world as we variously experience it: bringing an exacting eye, taut rhythms and often vivid language to our subjectively skewed perspectives.

19. A formalist, often adapting traditional forms such as sonnets and sestinas to (the poet's) own gender-bending sexual politics.

20. Their poems are intellectually challenging, at times arcane, though often written in populist forms such as ballads, folksongs or rhyming quatrains.

21. Exploring issues of identity in taut, lyrical style, the poet combines an acute ear for the music of life with a painterly eye for its most revealing details.

22. Enjoying the sounds and shapes of language for its own sake, this poet uses the medium to create a poetry as rich and sensuous as chocolate mousse.

GLOSSARY

ALLITERATION – the repetition of consonants at the start of neighbouring words in a line

ANAPAEST - a three beat pattern of syllables, unstress, unstress, stress. E.g. 'on the moon', 'to the coast', 'anapaest'

ANTITHESIS - the use of balanced opposites

APOSTROPHE – a figure of speech addressing a person, object or idea

ASSONANCE – vowel rhyme, e.g. sod and block

BLANK VERSE – unrhymed lines of iambic pentameter

BLAZON – a male lover describing the parts of his beloved

CADENCE – the rise of fall of sounds in a line of poetry

CAESURA – a distinct break in a poetic line, usually marked by punctuation

COMPLAINT – a type of love poem concerned with loss and mourning

CONCEIT – an extended metaphor

CONSONANCE – rhyme based on consonants only, e.g. book and back

COUPLET – a two-line stanza, conventionally rhyming

DACTYL – the reverse pattern to the anapaest; stress, unstress, unstress. E.g. 'Strong as a'

DRAMATIC MONOLOGUE – a poem written in the voice of a distinct character

ELEGY – a poem in mourning for someone dead

END-RHYME – rhyming words at the end of a line

END-STOPPED – the opposite of enjambment; i.e. when the sentence and the poetic line stop at the same point

ENJAMBMENT – where sentences run over the end of lines and stanzas

FIGURATIVE LANGUAGE – language that is not literal, but employs figures of speech, such as metaphor, simile and personification

FEMININE RHYME – a rhyme that ends with an unstressed syllable or unstressed syllables.

FREE VERSE – poetry without metre or a regular, set form

GOTHIC – a style of literature characterised by psychological horror, dark deeds and uncanny events

HEROIC COUPLETS – pairs of rhymed lines in iambic pentameter

HYBERBOLE – extreme exaggeration

IAMBIC – a metrical pattern of a weak followed by a strong stress, ti-TUM, like a heart beat

IMAGERY – the umbrella term for description in poetry. Sensory imagery refers to descriptions that appeal to sight, sound and so forth; figurative imagery refers to the use of devices such as metaphor, simile and personification

JUXTAPOSITION – two things placed together to create a strong contrast

LYRIC – an emotional, personal poem usually with a first-person speaker

MASCULINE RHYME – an end rhyme on a strong syllable

METAPHOR – an implicit comparison in which one thing is said to be another

METAPHYSICAL – a type of poetry characterised by wit and extended metaphors

METRE – the regular pattern organising sound and rhythm in a poem

MOTIF – a repeated image or pattern of language, often carrying thematic significance

OCTET OR OCTAVE – the opening eight lines of a sonnet

ONOMATOPOEIA – bang, crash, wallop

PENTAMETER – a poetic line consisting of five beats

PERSONIFICATION – giving human characteristics to inanimate things

PLOSIVE – a type of alliteration using 'p' and 'b' sounds

QUATRAIN – a four-line stanza

REFRAIN – a line or lines repeated like a chorus

ROMANTIC – A type of poetry characterised by a love of nature, by strong emotion and heightened tone

SESTET – the last six lines in a sonnet

SIMILE – an explicit comparison of two different things

SONNET – a form of poetry with fourteen lines and a variety of possible set rhyme patterns

SPONDEE – two strong stresses together in a line of poetry

STANZA – the technical name for a verse

SYMBOL – something that stands in for something else. Often a concrete representation of an idea.

SYNTAX – the word order in a sentence. doesn't Without sense English syntax make.

TERCET – a three-line stanza

TETRAMETER – a line of poetry consisting of four beats

TROCHEE – the opposite of an iamb; stress, unstress, strong, weak.

VILLANELLE – a complex interlocking verse form in which lines are recycled

VOLTA – the 'turn' in a sonnet from the octave to the sestet

Recommended reading

For the committed reader, there's a brilliant overview of developments in English poetry in Part 2 of *The Oxford English Literary History, volume 12,* by Randall Stevenson.

More general books on writing, reading & analysing poetry:

Atherton, C., Green, A. & Snapper, G. *Teaching English Literature 16-19.* NATE, 2013

Bowen et al. *The Art of Poetry, vol.1.* Peripeteia Press, 2015

Brinton, I. *Contemporary Poetry.* CUP, 2009

Eagleton, T. *How to Read a Poem.* Wiley & Sons, 2006

Fry, S. *The Ode Less Travelled.* Arrow, 2007

Heaney, S. *The Government of the Tongue.* Farrar, Straus & Giroux, 1976

Herbert, W. & Hollis, M. *Strong Words.* Bloodaxe, 2000

Meally, M. & Bowen, N. *The Art of Writing English Literature Essays,* Peripeteia Press, 2014

Maxwell, G. *On Poetry.* Oberon Masters, 2012

Padel, R. *52 Ways of Looking at a Poem.* Vintage, 2004

Padel, R. *The Poem and the Journey.* Vintage, 2008

Paulin, T. *The Secret Life of Poems.* Faber & Faber, 2011

Wolosky, S. *The Art of Poetry: How to Read a Poem.* OUP, 2008.

About the authors

An experienced Head of English and freelance writer, **Neil Bowen** has a Masters in Literature and Education from Cambridge University and he is a member of Ofqual's experts panel for English. He is the author of *The Art of Writing English Essays for GCSE and* co-authored *The Art of Writing English Essays for A-level and beyond* and *The Art of Poetry series, volumes 1-8*. Neil runs the peripeteia project linking A-level to university study of English: www.perirpeteia.webs.com

Head of A-level English, **Michael Meally**, holds an MA in American Literature as well as degrees in English Literature and Engineering. Michael's literary interests include detective/crime fiction, postcolonial literature and Greek tragedy. He is the co-author of *The Art of Writing English Literature Essays for A-level and Beyond* and *The Art of Poetry, volumes 1-4*. Michael writes regularly for the English & Media Centre magazine.

Johanna Harrison studied English Literature at Regent's Park College, Oxford University, writing her dissertation on Benjamin Britten's post-war opera libretti. Now a professional opera singer, she is currently studying at the Guildhall School of Music and Drama.

Answers to critical soundbites:

1. Barber
2. Dunmore
3. Heaney
4. Turnbull (about his own poetry)

5. Thorpe
6. Flynn
7. O'Driscoll
8. Nagra
9. Ford
10. Motion
11. Jenkins, quoting Virginia Woolf's father

12. Morrissey
13. Doshi
14. Feaver
15. Impostor: Boyle (not in this new selection)
16. Burnside
17. Armitage
18. Copus
19. Agbabi
20. Duhig
21. Fanthorpe
22. Impostor 2: Made-up comment on made-up poet.

Critical soundbites adapted from:
https://literature.britishcouncil.org
http://www.toppingbooks.co.uk
http://www.poetryfoundation.org
http://www.theguardian.com

18660268R00089

Printed in Great Britain
by Amazon